Thank You Ann Hupp
And You, Too, Samuel Brady

The Settlers' Forts of Western Pennsylvania

John A. DeMay

Printed by
Closson Press
1935 Sampson Drive, Apollo, PA 15613-9208
Library of Congress #97-91858
ISBN #0-9660243-0-3
Second Printing
September 1997
© copyright, May 1997
John A. DeMay

THANK YOU

The Author wishes to thank the many persons whose cooperation, assistance, and encouragement have contributed to the successful completion of this book:

Helen Louise DeMay, my wife, who joined me on many exploratory ventures searching for fort-sites and who gave me constant encouragement to complete this book.

Dennis B. Ardinger
Raymond Bell
Bruce Bomberger
Anna Lou Burig
Timothy Burke
Sylvester Casciola
Herb Clevenger
Ann Connor
Harold Cypher
Kim Darragh
Carol DePaul
Lonnie Doman
Ronald Eisert
J. Paul Fallon
George Finger
William Frankfort
Ray Johnson
Edie Jones
Joseph Joplin
Roy Keenan
Mable Kennell
Betty Koch
William Lane

Art Louderbach
Craig Moore
Erma Novak
Eugene Painter
Earl Petrucci
Zelda Rommes
John Roney
Dale Ruble
Eugene Ruperto
Jean Stout
Mary Ellen Todd
Daniel Todd
Melissa Todd
Thomas Todd
Matthew Todd
Robert Tohey
Anthony Vaccari
William Vogel
John Walbert
JoAnn Wetzel
Theresa Wilton
Virginia Wilton

Acknowledgments

The author gratefully acknowledges permission to quote from the following works:

John Bakeless. <u>America As Seen By Its First Explorers</u>. Dover Publications, 1961.

Allan W. Eckert. <u>That Dark and Bloody River</u>. Bantam, Doubleday, Dell, Inc., 1995.

Allan W. Eckert. <u>Wilderness War</u> (1978) and <u>Wilderness Empire</u> (1969). Little, Brown and Company.

Joseph J. Kelley, Jr. <u>Pennsylvania: The Colonial Years, 1681-1776.</u> Bantam, Doubleday, Dell, Inc. 1980.

Glenn D. Lough. <u>Now And Long Ago</u>. 1969.

Charles Morse Stotz. <u>Outposts of the War for Empire</u>. Historical Society of Western Pennsylvania, 1985.

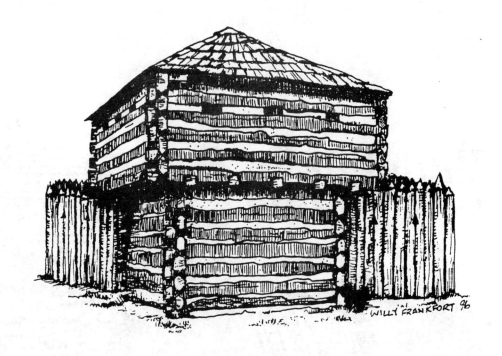

A blockhouse - the staple of frontier defense. Above is the view from the outside and below is an interior view. It is from such a structure as this that Ann Hupp fought.

This drawing, and that on the next page, are by William Frankfort, an expert on frontier life.

This shows a cabin built into the stockade wall at a blockhouse. There would have been as many of these small dwellings as there were families to be accommodated - usually three or four.

Frontier
Family
At
Home

Warriors

This man, at Bushy Run Battlefield, demonstrates the manner of dress and body painting of an Indian warrior.

A Shawnee Indian at Prickett's Fort with his war-club and tomahawk. Below is a Delaware warrior at Bushy Run Battlefield. The manner of painting the face and body was individual to each man and had significance to him. This painting was very important, almost ritualistic in nature, and was always done in preparation for fighting and usually done on ceremonial occasions.

The white shirt on the Shawnee shows the European trade influence.

Rangers

These men had the job of patrolling their neighborhoods looking for "sign" of Indian war-parties and then warning the settlers to "get to your forts."

They fought any Indian warriors they encountered and were responsible for trying to rescue captives. Needless to say it was a very hazardous life.

TABLE OF CONTENTS

Richard Gaetano   Albert Miller   John DeMay

Richard Gaetano was a History teacher in the Bethel Park School District. Now retired, he is actively involved in the study of frontier days in Western Pennsylvania.

Albert Miller is the discoverer of the Meadowcroft Rock Shelter outside of Avella. He is responsible for interesting the great archeologist, Dr. James Aldovasio, in the site as a result of which Dr. Aldovasio conducted extensive archaeological studies. It is now internationally known and has established the presence of Native Americans in this area fourteen thousand years ago - much longer than any other site in North America.

Mr. Miller also co-founded Meadowcroft Museum of Rural Life, commonly known as Meadowcroft Village, presently operated by the Historical Society of Western Pennsylvania. He is an avid historian of frontier life in this region and a member of many historical societies.

John DeMay is a retired attorney whose avocation has been the study of Native American culture and the conflicts between those people and white European immigrants. He has written magazine articles about those conflicts and belongs to several historical societies.

The existence of settlers' forts as a defense against Indian raids is well-known to historians. What is not well-known is the location of many of them and where one could find them today. We decided to try to fill this gap. It soon became apparent that there were so many of these forts - strung out along the creeks and streams of this region every two or three miles - and that their precise location was so difficult to determine that, for reasons of both time and energy, we had to establish geographic limitations. Thus is was that we selected western Allegheny County and northern Washington County as the main focus of our search. We have succeeded in locating thirty forts.

In our research we placed reliance upon the early writing of Rev. Joseph Doddridge "The Settlement and Indian Wars of the Western Parts of Virginia and Pennsylvania, 1763-1783," Earle Forrest's "History of Washington County," and the two-volume work "Frontier Forts of Pennsylvania." We also studied several other histories of Allegheny and Washington Counties, numerous historical pamphlets published by individual cities, boroughs and townships, and historical societies, and family genealogical studies that were kindly given to us by their authors.

We also discovered that often there was no documentation of the location of some of these forts. Then it was that we turned to, and relied on, the memories of Senior Citizens, some of whom are direct descendants of the fort -founder and who still live on or near the ancestral lands. Their bodies may be frail but their memories were clear and distinct. Some foundation ruins still existed in their youth (the 1920's and 1930's) and they knew the site very well. In addition they had parents and grandparents who had actually seen the structure-ruins in the period of 1870 - 1900, and told them about it and the exciting events that had occurred there.

It is our fond hope that others in surrounding counties will be inspired to make this effort in the area where they live. These forts were widespread in Greene, Fayette, Westmoreland, Washington, Allegheny, and Beaver Counties. It is very interesting, and a lot of fun, to try to find them and to discover the answer to the question, "What happened here?"

There are many interesting ones we could not find. Somewhere on Cherry Valley Road between Cherry's Fort and Burgettstown is Hoagland's Fort and just south of it is Allen's Fort. On Route 50 between Hickory and Avella are forts Milliken and McFarland, but where? Turner's Fort is just south of Rt. 22-30 and a few miles west of I-279, but we couldn't find it. Nor could we locate Montour's Fort at the junction of Montour Run and the Ohio River near the Greater Pittsburgh Airport; nor Beham's Fort near Eldersville and Mowry's Fort somewhere on Gilhall Road in Pleasant Hills, Allegheny County. We couldn't find them - why don't you try?

We also hope that, as to the forts we have identified, nearby historical societies and high schools will undertake the project of actually conducting an archaeological study to further confirm their existence and to see what material objects they may find. This should be done in coordination with the Pennsylvania History and Museum Commission in Harrisburg. These experts ought to be able to provide guidelines and standard forms regarding mapping the site, establishing a grid system, locating and identifying artifacts, and preserving and displaying them and writing reports about the search. Help also ought to be available from archaeological societies, especially for identifying artifacts.

We are well aware that the professionals dislike amateurs actually digging or metal-detecting at a site. However, these experts all lack the money, time, interest, and personnel to do it themselves. Something is better than nothing. Rather than let these sites pass into oblivion and be lost forever, it would be far better for the Pennsylvania History and Museum Commission, and the archaeological societies, to lend their assistance to an interested high school teacher and his or her curious and eager students or to the members of a local historical society.

So, here are the forts for you to learn about and the many hair-raising, exciting, and sometimes horrible events that occurred at each - as well as we could find them.

The reality of history can be disturbing, almost frightening. Sometimes we don't really dare to look at it "up close and personal." If we do, the view may destroy our comfortable myths and shock us. It's much easier to live with fond fallacies and delicate untruths. Sorry, you won't find those here.

This book is about the settlers forts that dotted the hills and valleys of Western Pennsylvania in the Olden Times. The period we speak of was brief as history goes - from 1760 to 1795 - but it was a terrible, fearsome, turbulent era. We can both be thankful that we skipped that chaos.

These forts were not military forts. They were very small, make-shift affairs that were built by and for the protection of only four or five families. Protection from whom? From the Native Americans, the Indians, who raided through this area very persistently in that thirty-five year period. They were quite nasty, to put it mildly.

The frontierspeople were farmers, each family owning a few hundred acres of land, and, of necessity, they were spread out and scattered. It was very easy for an Indian war-party to wipe out a family. To protect themselves a few of these settlers would get together and agree that since Sam Smith had a farm that was, roughly, in the center of their holdings, they would put their fort on his land. They would proceed to build either one extra-large cabin, or several small cabins near his house, and surround it and the necessary spring with a stockade fence. This would then be known as Smith's Fort, and when trouble came those families would rush there for safety - a process called "forting-up." There were scores of these small shelters, some primitive and others fairly elaborate, in western Pennsylvania in this era. This book locates and discusses the history of some of them.

It doesn't do, of course, to talk about settlers forts without discussing the settlers who built them. They were a unique people quite different from you and me. To tell the truth, I don't think you would like them at all; and, come to think of it, neither would they have liked us. I think they would disavow us as their lawful heirs. We are too rich, complacent, and meek for their tastes - pampered lap dogs to their lean and hungry wolves.

These were the people who founded our great country, mind you, and gave us the magnificent freedoms we so enjoy today. They were the men and women we honor and whose courageous achievements we proclaim in Fourth of July oratory. In truth they did all of the things our politicians praise, but - they were terribly rowdy, undisciplined, and, above all else, uncontrollable. They were boisterous, quite crude, very religious, and hard nosed

1

about it. No one ever gave them sensitivity training. Finally, they were a quarrelsome lot and loved hard liquor a little too much.

No, you wouldn't like them.

But we must talk about them - those determined people who built the forts and developed this land.

Ann Hupp and Sam Brady were two of those people; Ann a housewife and Sam a ranger or scout. They symbolize all of the frontierspeople of that time. Both lived a precarious existence and both were fighters. Brady's dangerous job was to go out looking for Indians, or looking for signs of them prowling around, and then to warn people like Ann and her family to get to their forts. Ann's job was to care for her family and, when necessary, to help fight the Indians. Ann, and the other women, fought with a fury, in their homes and front yards, and sometimes in hand-to-hand combat. Their lives, and that of their children, were in mortal danger and, if they had the chance, they used a rifle or tomahawk with deadly effect. Their kind of people won most of the time (but, just barely) and lost other times. When they won the Indians were driven away from their homes and they could get back to living again; when they lost they, and their children, died a horrible death.

We owe them a great debt of gratitude because most of the things we are - as Americans - are due to their struggle.

(Incidentally, if you are anxious about the matter the full story of Ann Hupp is in Chapter 5 and that of Sam Brady and his Rangers in Chapter 4.)

Since the Indians were the cause of this martial construction work we have to talk about them too. You wouldn't like them, either. Not many people did. They went out of their way to be obnoxious. Of course they were here first, if only by an historical eyelash, and they had their resentments. The men were warriors through and through, very arrogant, quite aggressive, boorish in their behavior, duplicitous. No one ever gave them sensitivity training either. In addition they had some nasty cultural traits of which three were their merciless killing, their love of torture, and their cannibalism. Oh - and they, too, loved alcohol. In fact, they were prime candidates for Alcoholics Anonymous. They were addicted to booze - man, woman and child.

As you can see these disparate peoples - the white Europeans and the Native Americans - were primed for conflict. Look at those characteristics again and tell me how they could possibly have gotten along. They couldn't. They didn't. One was looking for a fight and the other was glad to oblige. So we have to talk about their wars, and raids, and killing - a little, at least.

Finally, we have to say a few words about the land, the animals, and the politics of the day. Everything was different back then. The country was filled with endless forests, mountain lions prowled the hills ready to kill man or farm animal, and wolves howled at the cabin doors. Children were bitten by rattlesnakes.

The states were different - there was no Ohio nor West Virginia. Virginia claimed all of western Pennsylvania, and we nearly had a civil war over that. No one knew where the border was. Were Wheeling and Fairmont (now West Virginia) in Pennsylvania or did Virginia own everything up to Pittsburgh? The answer to that depended on whether you were a Pennsylvanian or a Virginian, and feelings ran high on the subject. Some of the settlers treated the whole area as a separate entity and there was talk of forming a state of their own!

Incidentally, Connecticut claimed the northern one-third of Pennsylvania - all the way across the state.

What a mess!

There were only a few counties in the state at that time. This entire area was called Westmoreland County, from Bedford in the east to the Ohio River in the west. The county seat was the tiny village of Hannastown, about three miles from Greensburg. It was burnt by the Indians (but has been re-built, recently, and you ought to go there some day).

Hardly any of our current cities and towns existed in those days.

The whole north-western part of our state from Pittsburgh to Erie remained Indian country until almost the end of this era, and was the last section to be settled.

Perhaps, above all, and most important, was the attitude of the settlers toward government and authority. Today we meekly submit to thousands of rules and regulations - we stop at red lights; we file our income tax returns by April 15th; we secure a license to go fishing and a building permit to construct a house. We abide by the rules of a myriad of agencies - HUD, OSHA, EPA, EEOC, one could go on and on. We are protected - securely protected - by local police, county police, state police, the FBI, DEA, ATF. Compared to the old days we are almost slaves to governmental authority and we are as safe as a babe in its mother's arms.

Back in the Olden Times - in Western Pennsylvania - there was no one to give you orders. No one at all. If by chance, a decree from Philadelphia, Williamsburg, or London came slowly drifting westward and into this land, it was scoffed at and ignored.

Most especially, there was no one to protect you. No one at all. In this wild land one lived or died according to his or her own strength and skill. There were no "cops" to call. If

3

you were on the frontier you farmed and fought alone - sometimes with the help of a very few neighbors. Is it any wonder that every man carried with him at all times a rifle, tomahawk, and knife, and that women and children learned to shoot a rifle as well as a man? These people were fierce and defiant because life made them so.

It was different back then. Keep this in mind as you read these pages.

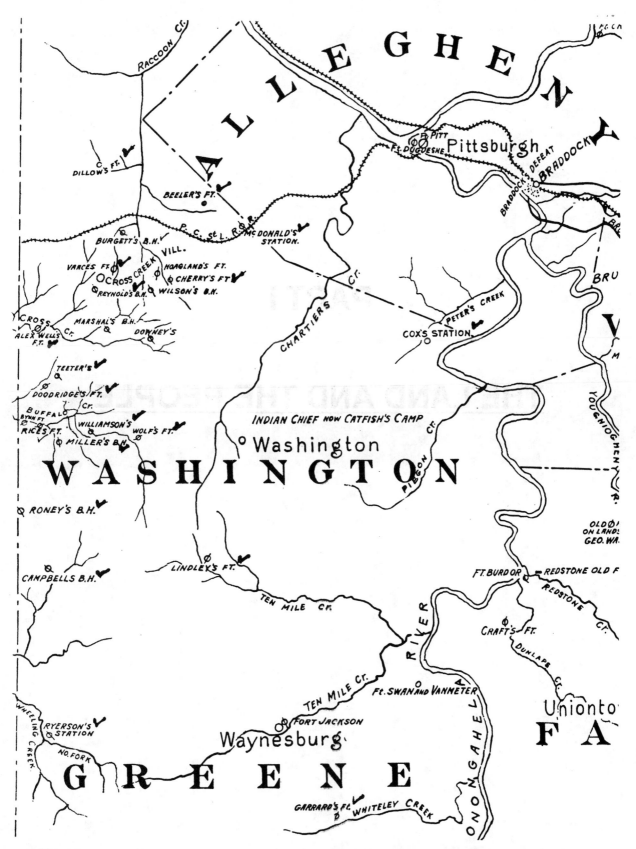

A portion of a map from the first edition of Frontier Forts of Pennsylvania showing some of the forts whose exact locations have been identified in this book. Note that they were nearly always constructed along streams.

PART I

THE LAND AND THE PEOPLE

Chapter 1

The Land

The woods were dark, mysterious, and deep. Usually there was no sound, nothing stirred. Occasionally a passing breeze would blow through the high branches and cause a half fallen tree to groan as it rubbed against a standing neighbor. Shadows flickered everywhere and sunlight barely sifted down through the cracks and creases of a million blocking leaves. A visitor - one strange to the woods - would get a panicky feeling that hidden eyes were watching with threatening intent.

The forests of Western Pennsylvania were a frightening place to civilized travelers from the east and never to be entered alone or without an experienced guide. Col. Bouquet, a British commander, once remarked, ruefully, that if he sent one of his red-coated Regulars off the road and one-hundred feet into the woods the man would get hopelessly lost.

The vastness of the forests excited comment from many observers. A German doctor, attached to the British army during the Revolution stated: "What I saw every day and in the greatest number was trees....from Carlisle it is not only continuous forest, but a very monotonous forest, there being little variety." [1]

An English settler observed: "There is too much woods, and, when on the barren peak of some rocky hill, you catch a distant view, it generally is nothing but an undulating surface of impenetrable forest." [2]

A more cheerful and appreciative view is expressed by Thomas Pownall, who spoke of an "Ocean of Woods swelled and depressed with a waving surface like that of the great Ocean itself." [3], and he enthused that:

> "If a Spectator hath gotten a stand on some high Mountain so as to look across any Number of the Ridges which may be less high than that he stands on, he then sees a repeated Succession of Blue and Purple parallel waving lines behind each other" and he thought these were "the most picturesque landscapes that Imagination can conceive." [4]

The underbrush in the forest varied from minimal to impenetrable. Listen to Thomas Ashe describe a portion of the woods through which he traveled:

> "The American forests have generally one very interesting quality, that of being entirely free from under or brushwood. This is owing to the extraordinary height, and spreading tops, of the trees; which thus prevent the sun from penetrating to the ground, and nourishing inferior articles of vegetation. In consequence of the above

circumstance, one can walk in them with much pleasure, and see an enemy from a considerable   distance." 5

And then there were places like Laurel Ridge, by Ligonier, where the scrub oak and laurel bushes were so thick as to be veritable walls. Thomas Pownall spoke of them: " The undergrowth towards and over this Hill is so abundant in Laurel Thickets that the Traveler must cut his way through them." 6

The gloomy aspect of the great forests and the frightening animals who roamed through them are specifically mentioned by Dr. Schoepf and also by Thomas Ashe who hated his nights in the mountains on his journey between Bedford and Pittsburgh. Said Dr. Schoepf:

> "In the eternal woods it is impossible to keep off a particularly unpleasant, anxious feeling, which is excited irresistibly by the continuing shadow and the confined outlook." 7

And Ashe commented with undoubted worry that: "Wolves, panthers (cougars), and tiger-cats (bobcats) were at hand to devour me." 8 Rattlesnakes were everywhere and constituted a special hazard. A hunter from Williamsport, Philip Tome, once saw: "...a pile of rattlesnakes as large as an outdoor bake-oven. They lay with their heads sticking up in every direction, hissing." 9

Still there were broad, fertile valleys, between the ridges, that interrupted the endless expanse of trees. "The glade between Allegheny Mountain and Laurel Hill was ten or twelve miles wide, filled with high, thick grass - fine fertile country of excellent meadowlands." 10 George Washington found another lush valley just east of Chestnut Ridge, near Uniontown, which he called the Great Meadows and in a part of which he put his little, aptly named, Fort Necessity. There were many of these meadows just waiting to be turned by the plow.

Throughout this vast stretch of forest, from the Allegheny Mountains to the Ohio River, the only means of travel was by Indian trails or the rivers. There were dozens of Indian trails criss-crossing the western part of our state. Continued usage made them well-worn, and well-known, but it must not be forgotten that they were paths. Indians habitually traveled in single file so that these trails were quite narrow traces winding through the woods. When the Indian acquired the horse (and, remember it was the Europeans who brought the horse to America) and used them for riding and packing their goods, the trails, inevitably, became a little wider. Still, horses were not in extensive use (the very nature of this forested country inhibited the development of large herds of horses) and the most common way to get from point A to point B was to walk. The Indians had no wagons so there was no need for broad paths.

The second means of transportation was to use the rivers. This was a great way to travel, if one were going north and south - for most of our rivers and creeks flow in those directions, but they provided little utility for east-west travel. It could be done, but it usually required a zig-zag course and back-breaking, time-consuming portages. If one wanted to go west, for example, one might have to get on a river and paddle north for some miles, then locate a tributary creek that headed northwestwardly for a distance, portage across country to another creek that proceeded southwestwardly, and eventually reach a river that flowed south until one arrived at ones (westward) destination. It sounds easy but it wasn't. Those "tributary creeks" had the bad habit of drying up or becoming very shallow in the summer months, and many water-routes were frozen in the winter.

French Creek in northwestern Pennsylvania is a good example of this proclivity. In its day it was an Interstate Highway. People coming from Erie would portage many miles to Waterford and get on French Creek at that point. Then they would drift down to Franklin, make a right turn on the Allegheny River, and go on down to Pittsburgh. (If they wanted to they could keep going down the Ohio to the Mississippi River, turn left, and go all the way to New Orleans.) But to get back to French Creek - this writer can personally attest that in July and August that stream can get ankle-deep in places, and no loaded canoe is going to get through. One either portages around the riffles or prays for rain.

In addition, just the mention of the word "portage" would evince a groan from every seasoned traveler. This meant pulling the canoes ashore, emptying them of all of their goods, carrying the canoes some several miles to the next creek, returning to the original site to load up with the goods, carrying those things to the new launch site, loading the canoes again, and then shoving off. It was always a headache.

All of this changed dramatically due to two British generals - General Edward Braddock and General John Forbes.

Everyone recalls Braddock's ill-fated expedition to capture Ft. Duquesne at Pittsburgh. This was the summer of 1755. In order to move his large army, with its many wagons, columns of marching Redcoats, and wheeled artillery pieces, Braddock needed a road. He put several hundred men to work cutting a twelve-foot path through these "impenetrable forests" from Cumberland, Maryland to Pittsburgh, and thus the first road in western Pennsylvania came into existence. Today that road, in general, is US Route 40 - our first National Road.

Braddock lost his fight (and his life, also) so the British tried again three years later. Now it was the turn of General John Forbes in 1758. He was coming from the east, and he, too, needed a road along which to march his army. While he was making his plans a tremendous argument arose within his staff about how best to get to Pittsburgh. Many officers, including George Washington, argued that it was foolish to cut a new road over the mountains and that it would be best to use the old Braddock Road, thus saving an enormous expenditure of time, labor, and money. Very happily for the people of Pennsylvania Forbes did not agree. He began his own road at Bedford and went straight west over the mountains, by-passing Edmond's Swamp, through the valleys and on to Ligonier, then to Pittsburgh. That road today is US Route 30 and it is a beautiful ride, if someday, you are looking for a day-trip.

These are the roads that opened up the settlement of western Pennsylvania. They were, for the times, two broad, majestic highways that made travel possible by wagon, coach, and teams of horses or oxen. The Braddock Road came up from the southwest, from Virginia and Maryland, and up this way came the Scotch-Irish peoples. The Forbes Road came directly across country from Central Pennsylvania and this road was used by the Germans, mostly the children of immigrants who had earlier settled in central Pennsylvania, and also those recent immigrants, often Irish, who had landed at the port of Philadelphia.

The movement of settlers into this country never occurred as a smooth, steady, continuous flow of people; quite to the contrary, it was a very episodic, jerky, on again -- off again, type of advance. It was entirely dependent on the purchase of lands from the Indians by the State, or earlier, by the Proprietors established by William Penn. All told there were eleven of these purchases beginning with land at and around Philadelphia in 1683 and ending with the purchase of a large part of northwestern Pennsylvania in 1785. It took one hundred years to buy up the whole state! 11

It is very interesting to observe that there was never any outright war-of-conquest against the Indians for this land. That could well have happened but it didn't happen. The pattern was established by William Penn - to his credit - to buy the land from the Indians rather than take it by force. This system worked fairly well except that serious arguments broke out among the Indians as to who owned the land, who had the right to sell it, and who got the proceeds.

After the state or the Proprietors got the land they would either sell directly to the citizens or sell huge tracts to a land company who would survey it, lay it out in lots, and sell them off. This was a profitable business.

Up until about 1750 the broad Susquehanna River, in the middle of our state, was the demarcation line between the white man and the Indian. West of that river was Indian country. That was the frontier.

Then came the great, climactic event that opened up settlement west of that river and over the mountains - it was the Treaty of Fort Stanwix (New York) in 1768. That treaty burst the dam, unlocked the gates, knocked down the wall - whatever - and allowed for the great influx of settlers into these western parts of our state. And, oh!, did they ever come. On the first day the Land Office was opened in Philadelphia, April 3, 1769, more than 2700 applications for this land were received. 12 George Croghan, a grizzled old trader who had been in these parts forever, it seems, must have been in a state of shock when he described what he saw:

"...but last year (1769), I am sure, there were between 4000 and 5000 (families), and all this spring and summer the roads have been lined with wagons moving to the Ohio." 13

This was written in 1770 and it was later estimated that "by midsummer of 1771...that there were ten thousand families in the upper Ohio country." 14 Considering the fact that a mere twenty years earlier there were no white settlers here and few Indians, that represents a dramatic change.

In 1770 George Croghan was the Superintendent of Indian Affairs in this area, and he had to have been overwhelmed by the changes he lived through. He was among the very earliest traders and spent many lonely days leading his pack trains through the dark woods on narrow trails to the Indian villages. Now, suddenly, this silent, primeval country was filled with people, axes felling trees, cabins being built, men out plowing their fields, children racing about, and scattered here and there, a church. In his lifetime this country had changed from desolate wilderness to civilization. He must have been awed by it all.

Once the settlers arrived in this area there were three ways to acquire land:

1. It was offered by the state as a reward for military service in the French and Indian War or some other official campaign. There were thousands of such claims filed by veterans of those several campaigns.

2. Buy the land. Pennsylvania opened up a land office in 1769 and sold the land for £5 per hundred acres up to a maximum of 300 acres. Even in those days they had "easy credit" arrangements. "Payment could be deferred until the patent was taken out - a process that could be stretched out for years." 15

3. A "Tomahawk claim." The earliest settlers - the unruly ones who "jumped the gun" and came out here long before 1768 (when they had no business being here)

simply chose the site that they wanted, then walked the perimeter hacking a distinguishing mark on trees as they passed by. This was known as a "tomahawk claim" and it was common and respected by the neighbors (who were doubtless doing the same thing).

It was completely illegal, caused quarrels with the Indians, and in later years, terrible migraine headaches to judges, lawyers, and everyone else concerned with land titles including Land Office officials who never knew whether the land they were legitimately selling was already subject to some unknown "tomahawk claim." What a mess that caused. As one writer put it: " The settler who by his own toil and that of his family made a clearing, raised a crop, and erected a homestead pointed to these accomplishments and demanded that his rights be recognized. If the law did not protect him the stout arms of his neighbors and fellow squatters could be counted on to resist the claim jumpers." 16

Those "claim jumpers," of course, were those who legitimately purchased the land from the state.

In any event, there were so many settlers with "tomahawk claims" that adjustments were made and they were eventually recognized as legal claims and deeds (patents, back then) were issued.

Another nightmare was caused by the fact that while Pennsylvania was selling this land, Virginia was doing the same thing to the same land! Can you imagine the legal quagmire. One piece of property could be the subject of a tomahawk claim, a legitimate sale from the state of Pennsylvania, and an equally legitimate sale from Virginia. Then you would have three very angry property owners. Is it any wonder that fights broke out?

That actually happened when George Washington, George Rogers Clark, and Michael Cresap, an old trader, all claimed title to the same piece of land! There was a lawsuit over this and George Washington won. 17

All this came about because no one was sure of the boundary between the two states and which government had jurisdiction over which land.

To make matters worse - if that was possible - Virginia sold the land for a lower price than did Pennsylvania.

"In or about the year 1774, Governor Lord Dunmore (of Virginia) opened several offices for the sale of lands within the bounds of what are now called the four western counties of Pennsylvania (Fayette, Washington, Allegheny, and Greene). The warrants were granted on paying two shillings and six pence fees. The purchase money was trifling, being only ten shillings per hundred acres, and even that was not demanded. This was an effectual inducement to apply to Dunmore's agents, in preference to the Pennsylvania land office..." 18

Virginia also recognized tomahawk claims for farms up to 400 acres and issued deeds for them.

It was customary to give your property a name in those days and on every deed there is a line for your choice. Many of them were hilarious - James Dinsmore, filled with religious fervor and high hopes called his "Land of Canaan," and William Fife was obviously overjoyed with his choice naming it "Fife's Delight." John McCreary had a sense of humor with his "Good Entertainment." Some people weren't very optomistic - they apparently looked at the steep hills, the gullies, numerous rocks, and all the trees they would have to cut - and groaned. Adam Patterson came up with "Trouble Without Profit," Hugh Sterling called his "Small Hopes," while Joseph Philips used one word, "Ugly."

(We may fairly suspect that Patterson, Sterling, and Philips were among the first to leave and head for Kentucky!)

So this primeval land began to fill with settlers and farms. The cougars, wolves, elk, woods-buffalo, and deer slowly gave way to cattle, sheep, hogs, and chickens. A new county was created - Westmoreland County stretching from Bedford, across the mountains, and clear to the Ohio River on the west.

There was only one tiny problem with the "Land Rush" Treaty of 1768. It had been made with the Iroquois Indians and this land was the hunting grounds of the Delaware, Shawnee, and Mingo Indians. To add insult to injury, the Iroquois got the money - about £20,000, a quite substantial sum - while the others had to move.

Needless to say the local Indians were resentful. They didn't dare quarrel with the Iroquois - their masters - but they could, and did, bear a grudge toward the white people who streamed into this country.

About fifteen years earlier, around 1750 or so when the French and English both claimed the land, one observer talked with a Delaware chief and then wrote this interesting note:

"The Indians were not well satisfied as to the rights of either the French or English. An old Delaware sachem exclaimed, 'The French claim all the land on one side of the Ohio, and the English on the other; now where does the Indian land lie?'."

That was a fair question.

Our observer goes on to remark with some irony: "Poor savages! Between their Father, the French, and their Brothers, the English, they were in a fair way of being lovingly shoved out of the whole country." 19

He neglected to mention their Uncles, the Iroquois, who did nothing in a loving manner where other tribes were concerned. They claimed ownership of the land, they sold it, and then they told the Delaware and Shawnee to "get out and get out fast." Those Indians left. For some of them this was the second or third move in their lifetimes at the orders of the Iroquois. When the Penns landed at Philadelphia in 1683 they found the Delawares along the Atlantic coast; eighty-five years later, in 1768, they were in Ohio.

George Croghan wasn't the only one who must have gasped at the great changes that can occur in a lifetime.

NOTES

One: THE LAND

1. John Bakeless, *America As Seen By Its First Explorers* (New York, NY: Dover Publications, 1961), p. 271.
    This is a fascinating book depicting the vast changes in the plants and wild animals of a few hundred years ago and today. For example, fish were monsters by our standards and routine wild-life included buffalo, elk, wolves, cougars, and wildcats, now disappeared from the woods of Pennsylvania.
2. Ibid., p. 271.
3. Ibid., p. 279.
4. Ibid.
5. Ibid., p. 272.
6. Ibid., p. 278.
7. Ibid., p. 272,
8. Ibid., p. 273.
9. Ibid., p. 275.
10. Ibid., p. 279.
11. Joseph J. Kelley, Jr., *Pennsylvania: The Colonial Years, 1681-1776* (Garden City, NY: Doubleday & Company, Inc., 1980), p. 394.
12. Ibid., p. 669.
13. Solon J. Buck and Elizabeth Hawthorn Buck, *The Planting of Civilization in Western Pennsylvania* (University of Pittsburgh Press, 1939), p. 144.
14. Ibid.
15. Kelley, p. 671.
16. Buck, p. 136.
17. Allan W. Eckert, *That Dark and Bloody River* (New York, NY: Bantam Books, 1995), p. 655, f.n. 125.
18. I.D. Rupp, *Early History of Western Pennsylvania* (Lewisburg, PA: Wennawoods Publishing, 1995; originally published, 1846, Harrisburg, Pa.), p. 46.
19. Thomas Lynch Montgomery (ed.), *Frontier Forts of Pennsylvania, Vol. II, 2d ed.* (Evansville, Ind.: Unigraphic, Inc., 1978, originally published 1916, Harrisburg, Pa.), p. 567.

Chapter 2
The Settlers

There was one group of white people who strode cheerfully through the dense woods with confident step and unerring direction. They were undisturbed by the silence, the darkness, and the wild animals, and not at all troubled by that "unpleasant, anxious feeling" that bothered Dr. Schoepf. They were the frontierspeople who were born and reared among these beautiful, often hostile, forested ridges and meadowed valleys.

What a strange, fierce people they were. It is said that the frontiersmen came over the Allegheny Mountains with a rifle in one hand, a Bible in the other, and a jug of whiskey over their shoulders. When they arrived along the Monongahela River, or a little further west, along the Ohio, they chose for themselves a likely piece of land, cleared it, built a small log cabin, then returned east for their wives and children. When they came back they settled in to farm this country. One observer noted, caustically: "They grew small crops of corn and large crops of children." This was obviously an effete, eastern snob who was shocked at the rough ways of these people for he, or she, added: "A kind of white people are found here, who live like savages," and that "they keep the Sabbath and anything else they can lay their hands on." 1

He, or she, clearly didn't like them.

They were a restless breed, these frontierspeople, independent , quick-tempered, defiant of all authority, and proud of their self sufficiency.

Necessity was a major cause of those attributes. The Rev. Joseph Doddridge grew up in this area during those wild times, and he wrote extensively about frontier life. He said:

"In the section of the country where my father lived (about 30 miles from Pittsburgh) there was, for many years after the settlement of the country, neither law nor gospel. Our want of legal government was owing to the uncertainty whether we belonged to the State of Virginia or Pennsylvania....

Thus it happened, that during a long period of time we knew nothing of courts, lawyers, magistrates, sheriffs, or constables. Every one was, therefore, at liberty to do whatever was right in his own eyes." 2

He points out that while they "had no civil, military, or ecclesiastical laws" nonetheless, amongst a sparse population where everyone knew everybody, "public opinion had its full effect and answers the purposes of legal government..."

Lord Dunmore, The British governor of Virginia, wearily observed their unrelenting thirst for new land and rebellion to all government. He was probably frustrated and tired when he wrote:

"I have learnt from experience that the established authority of any government in America, and the policy of Government at home, are both insufficient to restrain the Americans; and that they do and will remove as their avidity and restlessness incite them."

He goes on to add:

"They acquire no attachment to Place: But wandering about Seems ingrafted in their Nature; and it is a weakness incident to it, that they Should forever imagine that Lands further off are Still better than those upon which they are already Settled." 3

It is pertinent to note that Lord Dunmore knew whereof he wrote - many of the frontier people coming across the Allegheny Mountains into western Pennsylvania were his Virginians, supposed to be under his authority, and required to obey the statutes and regulations of both his government in Williamsburg and those of the King and Parliament in England. That they refused to do so caused him unending dismay and an infinity of problems.

In 1750, there were no white people living and farming in western Pennsylvania. A mere twenty five years before the Revolution, this area comprising Allegheny County, Washington, Fayette, and Greene Counties was lonely and desolate. A very few nervy, white traders led their pack trains along Indian trails through the woods, bypassing the swamps and steep hills, to the Indian villages along the rivers. Even the Indians didn't spread out and live within this land. The vast area between the mountains to the east and the Ohio River on the west was their hunting ground. They roamed through it but didn't live there.

"The region on or about the Ohio and it's numerous tributaries, was then only used as a hunting ground by the Mingoes and Shawanese Indians, and as a highway for parties at war of different nations, in their martial expeditions against each other. By reason of the unceasing hostilities between the more northern and southern Indians, these expeditions were frequent and tended to retard the whites from attempting to settle sooner. Near the junction of the Allegheny and Monongahela, no attempt was made to commence settlements till the Ohio Company made the attempt; till after 1758." 4

The white settlers were all east of the Susquehanna River, east of Harrisburg. The entire state was owned partly by the Indians, partly by the Proprietors (William Penn and his successors), and partly by citizens who had purchased their small parcels from the state (Proprietors). One may recall that the King gave land in Pennsylvania to William Penn (land which the King did not own) and that upon his arrival Penn bought the land from the Delaware Indians (land which they had no authority to sell). Then Penn sold off parcels of this land to settlers whom he and his successors recruited from Europe.

This became the accepted pattern for the acquisition and distribution of all land within the state.

In 1750 land west of the Susquehanna River was Indian land and no white person was allowed to own that land nor settle on it. Thus the problems began, because some white people - both native born and immigrants - refused to abide by those rules.

The situation becomes more complicated because of Indian politics - the tribes of the Iroquois Confederacy (The Five Nations, originally, and later the Six Nations: Senecas, Oneidas, Onandagas, Cayugas, Mohawks, and Tuscaroras) claimed that they owned the land rather than the Delaware or Shawnee tribes who resided on it, and no wise man ever took issue with the Iroquois.

Land was important because ownership of it was "the Goal - the Great Dream" of the European people who came to this New World.

Emma Lazarus had insight into both the historical fact and the souls of the immigrants when she wrote her famous ode to the Statue of Liberty:

"Give me your tired, your poor, your huddled masses yearning to   breathe free, the wretched refuse of your teeming shore.

Send these, the homeless, tempest-tost to me.

I lift my lamp beside the golden door."

That poem describes exactly the nature of our immigrants - "the wretched refuse" plus the tired, poor, and homeless. Those poor and homeless people wanted their own land more than anything else in this world.

Most of the immigrants came from England, Germany, Scotland, and Ireland. The vast majority were farmers with a few tradesmen and convicts thrown in for good measure. Nearly all of them were at the very bottom of the social scale in the "Old Country," so low that there were no human beings below them. Back "home" they were despised, deliberately oppressed, denied the most basic human rights, and they led miserable lives. A sign of their desperation was that most of them - to pay for their passage to America - sold themselves into a type of slavery, the "Indentured Servant" status. For five or seven years - it varied - they were almost slaves, sold to a master they had never known and forced to work for only food, shelter, and clothing, and you may rest assured, they got as little as possible of all three. There is very little discussion about this "white servitude" today, but in 1750 and beyond it was the most common way to pay for passage to the New World.

Benjamin Franklin estimated that between 1743 and 1763 "thirty thousand laborers, servants and redemptioners had come into the province" (of Pennsylvania). 5 By that time so many Irish had come that in 1729 the Assembly had laid a tax on their importation. 6 Between 1727 and 1750 a total of 134 immigrant ships arrived at the port of Philadelphia, alone, bringing about 27,000 people. 7

Pennsylvania avoided the importation of convicts from England (of whom about 18,000 were transported in the 18th century) initially by a statute prohibiting their importation. This was overruled by Parliament, but then the canny Quaker government imposed an import duty on them and required a ruinous bond on the importers and that did the job. 8 These convicts were, however, sent to Virginia and Maryland and it was from that direction that many settlers came into Western Pennsylvania.

Of these immigrants about one-third were German who, in America, were known to be honest, industrious and very progressive in their agricultural methods. Many of them had been solicited by pamphlets and agents of William Penn (one pamphlet was actually written by Penn). They were peasants and poorly thought of in the Rhine country from which they came. One jingle succinctly illustrates their status:

"The peasant could take the ox's place

Had he but horns above his face."

Another snide comment of the propertied classes was "...the peasant stands between the unreasoning beast and man." Finally it was observed by one author that "...many peasants lived in a kind of slavery...Often they are not as well off as cattle elsewhere." 9

It is breathtaking to imagine the feelings of these people when they finally arrived in Pennsylvania, worked off their indentureship, and then could get land for next to nothing in central Pennsylvania (the best farm land in the state as it turned out!), and with no one to rule their lives! To transform from a lowly despised peasant in Germany to a landowner in America and to be a completely free person on an equal plane with everyone around you had to have been an unbelievable, absolutely shocking and exhilarating experience. (That joy was shared by the Irish and Scotch peasants who came here in large numbers.)

These Germans settled in the southeastern and central parts of the state and they stuck together in small colonies primarily because of the language problems.

However, it was not they who became the settlers in Western Pennsylvania, but a more rough and ready breed, already acclimated to the forest, the hunt, and a certain restlessness - their children.

The Scots and Irish were as poorly treated in the Old Country as had been the Germans. Both were tormented by their English rulers and carried deep resentments across the Atlantic Ocean. Both came from the same island, the Scotch-Irish Presbyterians from Northern Ireland and the Irish Catholics from the south. Both suffered religious repression and their lifestyle has been described as "violent, squalid and mean." 10 The Irish Catholics were a little worse off since it was forbidden for them to own land or lease it for more than thirty-one years. Not only did the peasant have to pay exorbitant rent to his greedy landlord, but any improvements he made reverted to his "Lord of the Manor" at the end of the lease.11 The system was designed to crush a man and it worked very well. Sometime the overseer for the landlord-playboy in London would evict the tenant and raise large herds of sheep on the land - leaving the tenant and his family to wander the roads in a state of starvation.

The northern Scotch Irish weren't in much better condition. They have been described as "indifferent farmers, fierce in their Presbyterianism and fond of whiskey, they generally were restless and proud of their independent spirit." 12

Benjamin Franklin summed it up for all of the people in Ireland when he wrote:

"The English papers have of late been frequent in their account of the unhappy circumstances of the Common People of Ireland; that Poverty, Wretchedness, Misery and Want are become almost universal among them; That ...there is not Corn enough raised for their Subsistence one year with another; and at the same Time the Trade and Manufactures of the Nation being cramp'd and discourg'd, the laboring people have little to do, and consequently are not able to purchase Bread at its present dear Rate; that the Taxes are nevertheless exceeding heavy, and Money very scarce; and add to all this that their griping, avaricious Landlords exercise over them the most merciless Racking Tyranny and Oppression. Hence it is that such Swarms of them are driven into America." 13

Oh, unhappy Isle!

And come to America they did. It is estimated that 200,000 of them emigrated to America before the Revolution. Those who arrived in Pennsylvania found the land in the east occupied by the English and the Quakers, the center of the state filled with Germans but there, farther to the west, were vast beautiful, unclaimed lands where a man could take what he wanted, farm it and keep the products of his labor, and be free of all laws and rules and oppressive government. It was a lure that none could resist. "They were hard drinkers and hard fighters and when they wanted something nothing could turn them aside." 14 They could be "harsh, irascible, intolerant and restless, (but) they found the life of the hunter or the solitary farmer ideal, especially since they were also courageous, self-reliant, aggressive and hardy." 15

The Indians feared them. They came into western Pennsylvania from Virginia and Maryland by way of the Braddock Road and the Indians called them "the Long Knives." One Indian told James Smith, with regard to fighting the British or the Virginians, "The Indians said if it was only the red-coats they had to do with, they could soon subdue them, but they could not withstand Ashalecoa, or the Great Knife, which was the name they gave the Virginians." 16

They also had the Pennsylvania Rifle (which, mistakenly, has gone down in history as the Kentucky rifle). In their hands this was a deadly weapon and the frontierspeople became skilled by constant usage. During the early days of the Revolutionary War nine companies of frontiersmen from this area were sent to join the Continental Army around Boston and, from time to time, put on demonstrations of their shooting prowess. Dr. James Thatcher wrote, admiringly: "At a review... a company of them, while on a quick advance, fired their balls into objects seven inches diameter at the distance of two hundred and fifty yards." 17

That is very impressive marksmanship. It was impressive enough to be brought to the attention of the British Parliament during the early days of the Revolution. So many officers, sentries, and artillerymen were picked off at long range that Edmund Burke exclaimed in Parliament "your officers are swept off by the rifles if they show their noses." 18

Lest anyone think that the stories of their independence and aggressiveness are exaggerated it might be appropriate to tell a few stories about their conduct before they headed west over the mountains.

At one time the Susquehanna River represented the western border of the frontier, and Indians raided the settlers east of that river. The carnage was terrible. At that time Philadelphia was the state capital, the legislature met there, and the Quaker government, pacifist and self-righteous, refused to help the frontierspeople in any way. Despite their anguished pleas, the legislature refused to authorize money, powder, lead, guns, men, or equipment to help the settlers. In a rage, some fifteen hundred of those men - known as the Paxton Boys and their followers - set out to attack Philadelphia! Fifteen hundred very tough and very angry frontiersmen was not a force to be ignored. One of them composed a little ditty, directed at the Quakers in Philadelphia:

"Go on, good Christians, never spare

To give your Indians clothes to wear;

Send 'em good beef, and pork, and bread,

Guns, powder, flints, and store of Lead,

To shoot your neighbors through the head." 19

While the Paxton Boys and their followers advanced, a Quaker merchant went out to see where they were and he met a friend of his near Lancaster who advised him that these angry men were "the Scotch-Irish, along the Susquehanna who were of the same spirit with the blood-ran, blood-thirsty Presbyterians, who cut off the head of King Charles I," and that they were near by. 20

In great excitement the Quaker raced out of town and back to Philadelphia to spread the awful news. His message caused hysteria, pandemonium, and a general uproar. All hell broke loose! Church bells pealed, messengers raced their horses hither and yon through the streets and endless meetings were held of the legislature and City Council. Quakers had always proudly proclaimed their pacifism and were fond of lecturing the frontierspeople to be kind to the Indians and to disavow fighting as a means of resolving their problems. Now, with a raging fighting force on its way to their city - and themselves as the target - they suddenly forgot the power of "love and kindness," developed an admiration for muskets, and showed up carrying guns and hastily organized themselves into military units. (When this was reported to the invading frontiersmen it brought forth howls of derision.) Artillery was wheeled into place in public squares and aimed down the roads from which the frontiersmen might approach. Crowds roamed the streets, searching for news and spreading rumors.

At the ungodly hour of 2 AM on Monday, February 6, 1764, the city was awakened to "the clanging of fire-bells and the repeated roll of drums." 21 The dreaded moment had arrived! Every house in the darkened city immediately lit up as the citizenry put candles at the windows - per official instructions - to light the streets so that the newly formed militia rushing from their beds and into the roadways could find their way to their assigned positions. The clanging of the bells, the roar of the drums, and the pell-mell rushing about went on till dawn.

Among those dashing through the streets was a very worried Governor with his counselors and they headed straight for the house of Benjamin Franklin.

It is a shame that few of us know enough about Ben Franklin nor give him the great credit he deserves for being a leader and patriot. We see him in the paintings - an older man, wearing spectacles on a kindly face, sizable paunch showing beneath his vest, and always holding some paper to show his erudition. In point of fact he was a brilliant man, very understanding of the foibles of human nature - and he had the blessed gift of wisdom. Why else would the Royal Governor be racing for his house in the dead of night? Franklin had two more qualities - in common parlance he had guts and nerves of steel. In later years, during the American Revolution, when the representatives of the states bickered and threatened to go their separate ways he quietly, and chillingly, remarked "Gentlemen, we had better all hang together or we will most assuredly hang separately." He was a very practical man.

It was the next day - Tuesday - that Franklin rode out of town at the head of a delegation to meet the wild backwoodsmen.

As it happened he used his considerable diplomatic skills to quiet them, then arranged for a delegation to come into town to present their just complaints to the Governor and the General Assembly.

The revolt petered out and the Paxton Boys went back home. This was in 1764. Four years later, in 1768, it would be these men who poured across the Allegheny Mountains into western Pennsylvania, and eleven years later, in 1775, it was again these men who partook of another revolt - the American Revolution.

Sometime later, Franklin the Realist, laughed at it all - and at himself - when he recalled:

"The Proprietary Governor...did me the Honour, on an Alarm, to run to my house at Midnight, with his Counselors at his Heels, for Advice, and made it his Head Quarters for some time; And within four and twenty Hours, your Old Friend was a common soldier, a Counselor, a kind of Dictator, an Ambassador to the Country Mobs, and on their Returning home, Nobody again." 22

One might reflect that with a man like Benjamin Franklin as one of our Founding Fathers and the frontiersmen behind him, it is small wonder that we, finally, won that Revolution. What a striking combination they were!

This threatened attack on Philadelphia by the Paxton Boys and their followers clearly demonstrates the audacity, defiance, and aggressiveness of these "backwoods" people. Just keep in mind that Philadelphia was the largest city in America at that time with a population of 25,000 people. It was the state capital and did have a contingent of Royal troops stationed there. It is outrageous to think that it would, or could, be attacked by a mere fifteen hundred men - but those men were willing to try. They dared to be different - and difficult.

Another illustration of the unruly nature of the frontierspeople is a story about the audacious conduct of The Black Rifle and his Black Boys.

James Smith was 18 years old when he volunteered to go with General Braddock on his ill-fated mission against Ft. Duquesne at (now) Pittsburgh. General Braddock was marching his men through the thick unending forest and he needed a road. Smith was one of hundreds who were sent far in advance of the army to cut trees and clear a road about twelve feet wide. It had to have been tedious, back-breaking labor. Hostile Indians were constantly lurking about and one day Smith was captured. After enduring the usual beating (often deadly) by "running the gauntlet" at every village through which he passed, he was finally adopted into the Coughnawago tribe - an off-shoot of the Mohawks. He lived with them for several years but saw his chance to escape one day and did so.

He returned to his friends along the frontier which was then around Bedford, just east of the Allegheny Mountains. A few years later Indian raids began again in earnest and that is when he organized his Black Boys. He dressed them as Indians, they painted their faces and bodies in red and black war paint, he taught them Indian tactics, and they became much-admired "saviors" among the farm families whose homes and persons were being attacked. They were very much a "reactive" force. They did some patrolling throughout the neighborhood looking for signs of Indians, but mostly they were at their farms until they saw smoke in a valley rising from the burning house of a distant neighbor or an hysterical child came riding up to announce the massacre of his or her family. Then the Black Boys gathered and went out in search of the Indian raiders, stopping only to look for survivors around burnt-out cabins and to bury the dead of a family they knew. They were very successful in tracking down these raiding Indians, fighting them, driving them away, and recapturing prisoners.

Among the persons the settlers hated - and their ill-feelings encompassed Indians, Quakers, magistrates - were traders who sold guns, lead, and powder to the Indians.

On one occasion Smith learned of a pack train coming though the mountains loaded with just such merchandise. There were eighty-one horses in this train so it was a large one. Smith rounded up ten of his Black Boys and ambushed the traders on Sideling Hill. The Pennsylvania Turnpike goes over that mountain today not far from the scene of this ambush. The Black Boys destroyed sixty-three horse loads of goods, Smith proudly recounted, burning the guns and powder, spilling some rum and allowing the traders to go back with only a few horse loads of blankets and other innocuous goods. The traders did go back, to Fort Loudon, near Chambersburg. This was a military fort, garrisoned by Highlanders of the famous Black Watch Regiment. It was on the frontier and represented the power and might of the State and

Royal authority in the area. The garrison commander, Capt. Grant, was not only a military leader but the very representative of government in both civil and criminal matters. There was no one else to perform those functions except him.

The traders reported the outrageous events to him and, quite properly, he set out to apprehend the culprits. Not so surprisingly he couldn't find any person who would either admit to being a part of the Black Boys or knowing about the ambush and destruction of the trader's goods. In exasperation he arrested eight "suspicious" persons and jailed them in the fort. That was a mistake. The news flew throughout the countryside and every farmer, with his grown sons, for a radius of thirty miles joined with Smith's Black Boys and headed for Fort Loudon. Nearly three hundred men encamped on a hill and besieged the fort. Capt. Grant tried to ignore the threat and kept his men on their regular duties both inside, and unfortunately, outside the fort. In ones and twos these Highlanders were kidnapped by the watching frontiersmen until they had twice as many prisoners as the good Captain had.

This was clearly an unacceptable state of affairs and there was absolutely nothing the commander could do. He certainly was in no condition to fight with these people.

He called a truce. There was a prisoner exchange. The settlers went home, happy. What Capt. Grant felt is unknown but may be guessed.

This incident reverberated across the state and soon the Governor, Attorney General, and other nervous officials hurried to nearby Carlisle to do something about this terrible defiance of the authority of both the State and the King.

Are you surprised to learn that:

"Although the Governor huffed and puffed and issued warrants for the arrest of some of the "Black Boys," no one would execute the warrants, and a grand jury...listened to witnesses but decided the testimony was too flimsy to return indictments." 23

My, my...

The excitement died down but Capt. Grant seemed to have learned nothing from the experience. He apparently had a short memory and a thick skull. Sometime later he seized some rifles from a few of the country people on a belief that they were stolen and, despite warnings to return them, refused to give them up. Once again Smith and his Black Boys had their way - they kidnapped Capt. Grant! The rifles were returned.

Then there is the story of Lazarus Stewart. A magistrate, for just cause, sent out a constable to arrest Stewart. Stewart was served with the warrant then proceeded to demolish the constable. Not content with that he strode into town and chased after the magistrate who flew for safety to his home where he locked and bolted the door and cowered inside. Stewart, with a pistol in his belt and a club in his hand, strode back and forth thundering for the magistrate to come out and arrest him. This, that wise man was not about to do. Eventually Stewart got tired, mounted his horse and went home.

His neighbors cheered his actions. 24

We see here two things - one, the wild, unruly, uncontrollable temperament of these German, Scotch-Irish, Irish, and English frontiersmen and, secondly, although this incident occurred in 1765, ten years before the Revolution, it shows the early growth of the seeds of Rebellion. Recall again the words of Lord Dunmore:

"I have learnt from experience that the established authority of any government in America, and the policy of Government at home, are both insufficient to restrain the Americans..." 25

Today we profess to admire these frontiers people for their courage, audacity, and aggressiveness. At Fourth of July celebrations across the land we cheer and praise these hardy pioneers. The President of the United States, Governors, Senators, and our local Mayors give speeches honoring these people who "made our country great and our freedoms possible." Do they mean it? Do they really know these people? Do they truly approve the wild, anti-government, anti-social behavior of the pioneers? Do you?

Were these things to occur today - in the area where you live, what would you say? There is a great deal of hypocrisy as we applaud the daring deeds of the men and women who gave us these United States with its Bill of Rights, Constitution, and liberty that is the envy of all other peoples in this world.

But, how would you react, today, to:

An armed mob threatening the state capital in Harrisburg;

Another armed mob laying siege to a large military base;

Kidnapping of senior military officers;

Kidnapping of US Army troops or those of the Pennsylvania National Guard;

Absolute defiance of statutes of the legislature in Harrisburg or the Congress in Washington;

The refusal of Sheriffs or US Marshals to serve lawful warrants;

The refusal of a citizens Grand Jury to indict in appropriate cases;

Attacks on sheriffs and judges.

I suspect you wouldn't like that. We both want to enjoy the benefits of freedom but we don't want the problems that went in to winning those rights. Today we want the gain but not the pain. Now that it's all over and someone else has paid the price, we can sit back and enjoy the benefits.

We have seen the audacity and aggressiveness of an Englishman, James Smith, and of a Scotsman, Lazarus Stewart, but we dare not ignore the Germans. They were a major component of the immigrants into western Pennsylvania. No story could be more appropriate than that of Frederick Stump:

It appears that one day four Indian men and two women came to his house. He claimed they were drunk and disorderly and when he told them to leave, they refused. Fearing for his life, he and an assistant, John Ironcutter, then killed them. They then went several miles away and killed some other Indians whom they suspected by being connected, somehow, to the group at his home.

There was a big "to-do" over this in Philadelphia. A warrant was issued for the arrest of the men and a group of soldiers nabbed them and put them in jail. It wasn't hard to do - Stump and Ironcutter were still at the house doing their daily chores as though nothing had happened. They were then to be taken to Philadelphia for trial instead of being tried in the county of their residence. That was another Big Mistake by the authorities. The settlers wanted to be tried in the county where they lived, not in Philadelphia by a jury of "damned" Quakers.

Stump's neighbors were upset. To begin with they had no objection to the killing of the Indians, and secondly, they believed that Stump would not get a fair trial in Philadelphia, and it set a bad precedent for themselves. So, as the Magistrate reported, this happened:

"...for about ten o'clock this morning there came, to the number of seventy or eighty men, under Arms, and who surrounded our Gaol, when a Number of them,...appears to have had but too ready entrance into the Dungeon, and in less than ten minutes time they carried off Stump and his Servant, in open triumph, and violation of the Law....The Jailor says that a pistol was held at his breast..." [26]

Stump and Ironcutter then disappeared but the government in Philadelphia was in an uproar over this matter. A reward was offered of £200 for Stump and £100 for Ironcutter. That was a very large sum of money for those days but the neighbors simply laughed at it and ignored it. A senior legislator wrote to Franklin:

" The Murderers are...at large and are escaped to Parts unknown out of the province. It is now near Two Months since the rescue and not a Warrant is issued against the rescuers, tho all well known to the Magistracy and Government, and might be easily apprehended." [27]

Interesting Discoveries

These are the ruins of the Smith cabin built about 1813. They stand along State Rt. 331 in Independence Township, Washington County, about one mile from Lamb's Fort. Notice the careful stone "chinking" between the timbers of the walls.

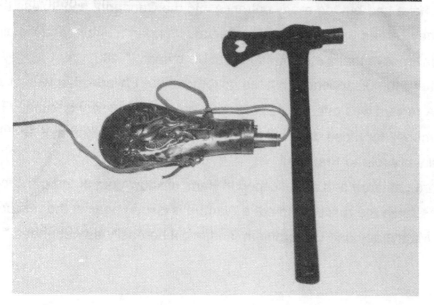

This metal, finely engraved powder horn belonged to a man name Jacob Cramer. He took the tomahawk from an Indian he killed. These are at the Washington County Historical Society.

Well, what can we say? The rescuers might have been well known but it would be like kicking a hornet's nest to try to arrest them. In any event, nothing was done. There was never any trial for this Great Escape or the killing of the Indians. As to Stump and Ironcutter, they had clearly left town and probably headed west into our end of the state.

To digress for a moment, these people didn't change when they came west. Move ahead to the year 1794: the Revolution is over; a United States Government exists, and that government has just imposed an excise tax on whiskey. It was "Philadelphia and the Paxton Boys" all over again. The great Whiskey Rebellion began! Government agents, the tax collectors, were shot at, captured, and "tarred and feathered." The house of John Neville, the Chief Inspector of the Excise, was attacked, set on fire, and destroyed. There was armed insurrection. President George Washington had to march 13,000 troops into Pittsburgh and environs to put it down.

Now that we have seen that frontierspersons of each nationality were equally capable of wild behavior, let us move on to the Grand Finale and see what they did as a group.

Nothing stopped these people, nothing at all. In 1750 no one was here in western Pennsylvania; by 1760 they had started coming in dribs and drabs - a few people here, a few people there. They moved slowly, west of Bedford, west of Fort Loudon. They crossed Laurel Ridge and Chestnut Ridge and settled near Ligonier, then toward Ft. Pitt. They moved toward Wheeling and began to settle around Brownsville, Uniontown, and Connellsville. They moved south of Fort Pitt into Bethel Park, Peters Township, Washington, and on west to the Ohio River.

We even know the names of some of these pioneers - there were so few of them. Christopher Gist settled in Mt. Braddock, near Uniontown in 1753 and he brought eleven families with him; Wendell Brown and several of his sons moved into Fayette County in 1751 or 1752; the Eckerlin brothers were into Greene County in the same years and William Stewart moved into Connellsville. Others - a very few others, - did the same.

The Indians protested bitterly and Col. Bouquet, in charge at Ft. Pitt, issued a proclamation in October, 1761 "prohibiting for the time being hunting or settling west of the mountains without a permit." 28 He went further, he actually sent out troops who burned the cabins and sternly ordered the farmers to go back east. These people sullenly watched the burning of their cabins, and, when the soldiers left, quickly re-built them.

The government moved to Step Two and took more drastic action. In 1763 came the great Royal Proclamation from London forbidding any settlement west of the Allegheny

Mountains. There was to be NONE, absolutely none! This was supposed to be the final word.

But, what can one do with people who believed that "...it was against the laws of God and Nature that so much land should be idle while so many Christians wanted it to labor and to raise their bread." 29

The Royal Proclamation did no good.

Then the frustrated government of Pennsylvania took desperate measures and, on February 3, 1768, passed a statute that decreed a PENALTY OF DEATH for settlers who had the nerve to cross the mountains and settle in these western lands. The statute is interesting. It states:

> "...That if any person...settled upon any lands within the boundaries of this province not purchased of the Indians by the proprietors...shall neglect or refuse to remove themselves and families off and from the said lands within the space of thirty days after he or she shall be required so to do...every such person...being thereof legally convicted by their own confession or the verdict of a jury shall suffer death without the benefit of clergy."

This is powerful language. It is clear, distinct, to the point, and has the awesome authority of the Commonwealth of Pennsylvania behind it. To violate that Statute was very serious business.

It did no good at all. The wild western citizens simply ignored it.

You couldn't frighten them with threats of death. They faced death every day - from Indians, wild animals, accidents, getting lost in the woods, starvation if their crops failed, from childbirth, from injuries, disease, and vicious fights among the men. You couldn't scare them - not against the allure of a beautiful piece of land to call their own and the chance to be totally free, way off in the woods.

It was no contest. They kept coming.

NOTES

Two: THE SETTLERS

1. Ray Allen Billington, *Westward Expansion* (New York, NY: The Macmillan Company, 1967), p. 93.
2. Joseph Doddridge, *The Settlement and Indian Wars of the Western Parts of Virginia and Pennsylvania, 1763 - 1783* (Bowie, Maryland: Heritage Books, Inc., 1988; reprinted in 1912, Pittsburgh, Pa; originally published in 1824), p. 130.
3. Joseph J. Kelley, Jr., *Pennsylvania: The Colonial Years, 1681-1776* (Garden City, NY: Doubleday & Company, Inc., 1980), p. 671.
4. I.D. Rupp, *Early History of Western Pennsylvania* (Lewisburg, PA: Wennawoods Publishing, 1995; originally published, 1846, Harrisburg, Pa.), p. 37.
5. Frank Ried Diffenderffer, *The German Immigration Into Pennsylvania* (Baltimore, Md.: Genealogical Publishing Co., Inc., 1979), p. 98.
6. Solon J. Buck and Elizabeth Hawthorn Buck, *The Planting of Civilization in Western Pennsylvania* (University of Pittsburgh Press, 1939), p. 127.
7. Diffenderffer, p. 102.
8. Joseph E. Illick, *Colonial Pennsylvania* (New York, NY: Charles Scribner's Sons, 1976), p. 114.
9. Ibid., p. 124.
10. Ibid., p. 120.
11. Allan W. Eckert, *Wilderness Empire* (Boston, Mass.: Little, Brown and Company, 1969), p. 18.
12. Kelley, p. 182.
13. Ibid., p. 183.
14. Buck, p. 132.
15. Ibid., p. 131.
16. James Smith, *Scoouwa: James Smith's Indian Captivity Narrative* (Columbus, Ohio: Ohio Historical Society, 1978), p. 118.
    This was originally published in 1799 as "An Account of the Remarkable Occurrences In the Life and Travels of Col. James Smith..."
17. Kelley, p. 732.
18. Lewis S. Shimmell, *Border Warfare In Pennsylvania* (Harrisburg, Pa.: R.L. Myers & Company, 1901), p. 73.
19. Kelley, p. 492.
20. Ibid., p. 494.
21. Ibid., p. 496.
22. Ibid.
23. Ibid., p. 546.
24. Ibid., p. 650.
25. Ibid., p. 671.
26. Ibid., p. 617.
27. Ibid., p. 619.
28. Buck, p. 102.
29. Ibid., p. 136.

Chapter 3
The Indians
I. The Good News

Today, most of the things we think about Indians (when we think about them at all) are wrong. We have some vague idea of a group of homogenous people (who they were we have no idea) who "lived here" (where "here" is we really haven't thought about) and who "owned" this land (although any self-respecting Indian would loudly proclaim: "What a silly idea - no one can own land; that is your crazy European Idea". Actually, European people had to teach the Indians the concepts of land ownership and property rights.) Then we dismiss the subject. We understand that there are Irish people and French and Spanish - and that each group has remarkably distinct, and different, characteristics but we never do the same for Indians. Mostly the cause is innocent ignorance. In point of fact, in this area where we live, there were Shawnee, Delaware, and Seneca who were just as different as the Irish, French, and Spanish. To add to the mix (and the problem) there were also wandering around your neighborhoods, Hurons, Twightwees, Ottawas, Mohawks, and periodically, some Cherokee, Catawba, and Mohicans. These were all Indians - or Native Americans - only in the same sense that the white people were all Europeans.

That really doesn't say much about them. At the least you have to appreciate the facts that they spoke in different languages, were widely scattered throughout our state and its neighbors, and they had varying customs and attitudes. They weren't all alike. Generally, they were similar; specifically each tribe was unique. They had deep hatreds for each other but were sometimes allied in a common cause and they were just as involved in internal politics and foreign diplomacy as were the white Europeans. It is difficult for many people to believe that they engaged in political bickering, heated arguments over tribal policy, and diplomatic intrigue with other tribes, France, England, and Spain, but it's true. They knew all the tricks, too, promises, threats, lies, deception and duplicity. It is absurd to think of these people as simpletons or naive savages taken advantage of by sophisticated white people. They were canny, sharp, and smooth in all of their dealings - whether over land purchases, trade, war, or relationships with other tribes. They knew exactly what they were doing and why.

Today ignorant persons often loudly proclaim "These Indians were just like us." That is not true. They were most definitely not "just like us." They would be offended by the suggestion. For your information they looked down upon us, didn't like us very much, and did their best to disassociate themselves from us. They loved our material goods but not our lifestyle. One Indian warrior remarked, caustically, "...that the white people appeared to them like fools; they could neither guard against surprise, run or fight." 1

They were a Stone-Age People just beginning to leave the "hunter-gatherer" stage of human existence and entering into the agricultural, small fixed village, phase of cultural development. To varying degrees, they did have subsistence farms and orchards , but women, alone, did whatever gardening was done. Men had not yet progressed to the point of being farmers. James Smith who was adopted into the Coughnawago band of Mohawk Indians was a strapping eighteen year old farm boy and once helped some women with their hoeing chores. He was severely chided by the men who told him "you must not hoe corn like a squaw." 2 These Indians could not read, nor write, nor do third grade arithmetic, nor build a bridge over a ten foot stream, much less a broad river. They had no Vienna Orchestra, nor a Mozart; there were no Michaelangelo sculptors, nor Raphael painters; no psalms by a David nor sonnets by a Shakespeare nor mathematicians like Euclid.

They were an extremely primitive people, expert at finding their way through our endless forests, superb hunters, and the men engaged in ceaseless war as a principal occupation.

Perhaps that very word "war" can be used to highlight one of the major differences between them and us.

We think of war as a major event. War is "declared," it involves the marshaling of great armies, climactic battles with terrible casualties, and, always a "just cause," i.e., "the glory of England," "to regain our rightfully owned lands in France," (or Spain, or Germany, or wherever), "to bring the great truths of Islam (or Christianity, or Buddha) to the Infidels."

How about war as a simple way of life? A routine occupation. One might ask a Seneca man "After you have brought home a few deer and bears from your hunting trip - enough to last your family for several weeks - what do you do with your time?" To which the answer would be: "Oh, I go on the war path against the Cherokee down in the Carolinas or the Hurons up in Michigan to see how many I can kill and to bring home a few prisoners to torture." "Well," one might go on, "do you do this often, and what is the purpose of this war?" To which the reply would be: "I do this all the time. This is what I do for a living, after hunting. And as to the purpose - it's fun. It's exciting. I love it. And, in addition, this is how I become an important man in my community. It's a prestige thing." Capt. Pouchot, the French commander at Fort Niagara noted: "...they cannot be happy without war. An Indian who remained three years without going to war would not be considered a real man and would suffer reprimands during their feasts." 3

War, or better yet, raiding, as a routine way of life, is a concept totally foreign to us. Even our professional soldiers only engage in war a few times in their careers. The very idea of going hunting in June and raiding in July, hunting in August and raiding in September - and doing this all of our lives, and just for the fun of it, is simply beyond us.

Yet, that was the lifestyle of the Indian man.

The women were "homebodies," engaged in the traditional tasks of bearing and raising children, making food and clothes, gardening and caring for the house. This was a matrilineal society in which kinship was traced through the mother and the women played an active role in the tribal government. It was pretty much a "behind the scene" role in that they participated in the councils within the village but rarely participated in the councils with strangers. Thus you had a Queen Esther and a Queen Aliquippa who were very much in charge within their villages but one doesn't read of their presence, or participation, in the numerous councils that were held with the British, French, or Americans. They were a power behind the throne, but always subservient to men.

On rare occasions Indian women did participate in councils with "outsiders." Louis Bougainville, a French officer, describes one such meeting which included twelve council women. "The council women were present at the sitting." And he goes on:

> "The sitting ended with the presentation of wampum belts to the council women. The gravity with which they attended the deliberations deserves to be noted. They have, moreover, the same standing among the Indians that the matrons formerly had among the Gauls and Germans." 4

While we may be ignorant regarding the status of "matrons" among the Gauls and Germans, we may rightfully assume that they were highly regarded and their views respected.

Mary Jemison, a white woman living among them observed:

> "The (male) Indians are very tenacious of their precedence and supremacy over their wives, and the wives acknowledge it by their actions, with the greatest subservience. It is a rule, inculcated in all tribes, and practiced generation after generation, that a squaw shall not walk before her husband or take the lead in his business. For this reason we never see a party on the march, in which squaws are not directly in the rear of their partners." 5

It is interesting to look at Indian life from an insiders point of view and Mary Jemison gives us that opportunity. Mary was captured at age 13 by the Shawnee and, after horrible experiences, was traded to the Seneca. She was adopted into one of the families and spent the rest of her life with them, had two husbands, and seven children. In later years she was called "The White Woman of the Genesee" and became very famous and well known. She dictated her reminiscences to an attorney-friend, Daniel Banister, who noted: "She speaks English plainly and distinctly, slightly tinged with the Irish idiom, and has the use of words so well as to render herself intelligible on any subject with which she is acquainted." 6 Her recollections were first published in 1824 and there have been numerous reprints. This is a testimony to her reliability and honesty.

She tells us that she became content among these people:

"With them was my home; my family was there, and there I had many friends to whom I was warmly attached in consideration of the favors, affection, and friendship with which they had uniformly treated me from the time of my adoption.

****

Our labor was not severe; and that of one year was exactly similar in almost every respect to that of the others.....

****

In the summer season, we planted, tended, and harvested our corn, and generally had all our children with us; but had no master to oversee or drive us, so that we could work as leisurely as we pleased.

****

In order to expedite their business, and at the same time enjoy each other's company, they all work together in one field, or at whatever job they may have on hand." 7

She notes that:

"Spinning, weaving, sewing, stocking knitting, and the like, are arts which have never been practiced in the Indian tribes generally." 8

She also tells us that "it is a fact that they are naturally kind, tender, and peaceable toward their friends, and strictly honest..." 9

The impressive fact about Mary Jemison is her candor and honesty - all was not "sweetness and light" in her relationships with her captors and she says so in no uncertain terms. One time she was taken to Ft. Pitt and she yearned to escape and to be liberated from the Indians. Then she was given to a warrior named Sheninjee to be his wife. She had no choice in the matter and it was fear that forced her to accept this requirement. As she says:

"Not daring to cross them or disobey their commands, with a great deal of reluctance, I went...." 10 She had seen their tortures, which she discusses frankly, and knew that if her family turned against her such a dismal fate was a real possibility. A few years later one of the chiefs decided he would take her to Ft. Niagara and turn her in to the British who were offering a bounty for prisoners. She had to go off into the woods and hide until this chief gave up the idea. It is evident that she was always "under a cloud" to some extent.

Another person who casts light on Indian life is James Smith who was taken prisoner when he was a mature eighteen year old. He was adopted into a branch of the Mohawk tribe and he, also, tells us that among themselves, these people were kind, considerate, sharing, and well-adjusted to their way of life. Amusingly, he points out that they could curse and swear as well as any white man and that while children were usually "ducked" in water for misbehavior, he did observe some spanking. Along with Mary Jemison he deplores the Indians' terrible addiction to alcohol and the truly awful fighting amongst themselves that it caused. Many people were killed and injured during these drunken orgies. Smith describes an actual council that was held to decide who among them could get drunk and who should stay sober! Then the sober ones removed all weapons from the designated drunks and tried to keep them from fighting and killing each other. He declares it to have been a terrible job. 11 Fr. Hennepin, a Catholic priest who lived among the Indians observed: "This traffic in strong drink was not agreeable to me, for if the savages drink ever so little, they are more to be dreaded than madmen." 12

Four years later Smith had had enough of Indian life, and when a good opportunity arose, he escaped and returned to his home.

Another aspect of Indian life that is always overlooked is the practice of both politics and diplomacy. In Indian villages the people voted on their choice of chiefs (can you imagine the "back-stage" maneuvering that went on? Maybe a little "gift giving" here and there?) and on whether to go to war with another tribe. The oratory was impressive and went on - not for hours - but for days!

The Indians seemed to love these gatherings, the speeches, and the haggling that was part of them. Their men made excellent, flowery speeches, quite colorful, invoking God, Peace, Friendship, Truth, and Duty, and everything was promised to last forever, " as long as the grass shall grow and the rivers flow." The great Greek and Roman orators would have loved them! They "pulled out all the stops" in those speeches; they would have done very well, and felt quite at home, in the British Parliament or on Capitol Hill in Washington. They were good at it.

A few illustrations are in order. (Note - in the primary source books these speeches go on for pages, only short excerpts are included here.)

After months of bloody raids on the settlers in Western Pennsylvania, Col. Bouquet gathered together a good-sized expedition - settlers and regular troops - and marched from Pittsburgh into Ohio. The Indians knew when to fight and when to quit (another judgmental skill they had which is often overlooked) so after they looked over this force (and they were aware of the fighting skills of Col. Bouquet) they called for a peace and Bouquet obliged. As part of the treaty the Indians were to stop raiding and deliver all prisoners in their possession to the English at Ft. Pitt. Guyasuta, a bloody Seneca chief, came in with some prisoners and made this speech:

"With this string of wampum, we wipe away the tears from your eyes....We gather together and bring with this belt all the bones of the people that have been killed during this unhappy war, which the evil sprit occasioned among us. We cover the bones that have been buried, that they may be never more remembered. We again cover their place with leaves, that it may be no more seen. As we have been long astray, and the path between you and us stopped, we extend this belt, that it may be again cleared, and we may travel in peace to see our brethren as our ancestors formerly did. While you hold it fast by one end and we by the other, we shall always be able to discover any thing that may disturb our friendship." 13

This was in November of 1764. Guyasuta would continue raiding for the next thirty years! So much for his idea of friendship. But, don't forget - he is trying to placate Col. Bouquet and get him on his way back to Ft. Pitt, and if a few sweet words will do it, fine. Note how he blames "the evil spirit" and that "we have been led astray" (No one ever "led" the Seneca anywhere - astray or otherwise) and, now that the raids are over, for a while, he says, smiling, "let's let bygones be bygones" - as if the settlers and soldiers could forget the recent murder of their women and children. He talks about an "unhappy war," but doesn't mention that it was all his doing!

In another speech some years later Guysauta brings the Lord into the picture and truly (he says) speaks from the heart:

" We have done our utmost to be ready to speak to-day as you desired; and we now inform you that it was owing to the nations who live to the westward of us, and to our foolish young men, that the war has happened between us, so that it is neither your fault nor ours..."

Notice how clever this is. The war with the English was caused by "nations to the West" and "foolish young men." Everyone is to blame but Guyasuta and the mature Seneca people. Note also that indirect suggestion that, just maybe, it was the English who might have been at fault.

Then he goes on:

"Brother: Now we have thrown away every thing bad, nothing remains bad in our ears; just good. We take fast hold of this chain of friendship, and we... request you will do the same, as we cannot hold it fast without your help, and we must both look up to God, who now sees everything that passes between us, for his assistance. Do not think that what we say comes from our lips only, it proceeds from the bottom of all our hearts; therefore we again request that you will join both hands with ours to this belt of friendship." 14

In point of fact Guyasuta had no heart at all when it came to killing white settlers or anyone else he didn't like or who offended him in some way, and he could be trusted about as far as you could throw him - and he was a very big man. But, he could make a good speech. He was very much a diplomat as well as a warrior.

Christian Post was sent by the government in Philadelphia into this area to try to re-establish good relations with the Shawnees, Delaware, and Mingo Indians in 1758. One chief, in council, addressed him, rather colorfully:

"Now, brethren, it is three years since we dropped that peace and friendship which we formerly had with you. Brethren, it was dropped and lay buried in the ground, where you and I stand, in the middle between us both. Brethren, I see you have digged up, and revived that friendship which was buried in the ground; and now you have it, hold it fast. Do be strong brethren, and exert yourselves that that friendship may be well established and strong between us."

***

"Brethren, when all the nations join to this friendship, then the day will begin to shine clear over us. When we hear once more of you, and we join together, then the day will be still, and no wind, or storm, will come over us to disturb us." 15

Finally, consider this portion of a speech delivered by a Delaware chief:

"Brother: I now gather all the bones of your deceased friends and bury them in the ground in the same place with ours so deep that none of our young people may ever know that misfortunes have happened between us....;

Brother: By this belt I also wipe away the blood, as you have done from the earth, and make your bodies quite clean, that you may appear to have as good hearts as those of your wise forefathers; and we hope what passes in this council will never be forgotten." 16

That was in 1768 and the Delaware kept up their raiding for about another 25 years.

These speeches were often so much fluff, designed to accomplish some specific purpose, but were quite colorful and held the attention of listeners. Indian orators do appear to have had one serious (and common) problem - they didn't know when to quit and sit down!

In all of these councils the Indians spoke in loud, clear voices with considerable variations in emphasis, cadence and tone so that the audience was held in rapt attention. Once they got on stage, so to speak, these speakers could disclaim as well as any Shakespearean actor. They were good at it. They may not have meant all they said but they sure sounded good. They were excellent diplomats.

Consider for a moment this admiring reaction of a frontier-officer to a speech by the great Shawnee chief, Cornstalk:

"When he arose and spoke he was in no wise confused or daunted, but spoke in a bugle voice that could be distinctly heard all throughout the camp, without stammering or repetition, and with peculiar emphasis. His appearance, while addressing Dunmore, made him the most dignified looking man I ever saw, truly grand and majestic, yet graceful and attractive. I have heard the finest orators in Virginia - Patrick Henry and Richard Henry Lee - but never have I heard one whose powers of delivery surpassed those of Cornstalk on this occasion." 17

All of these speeches were usually delivered to either the English military people or to representatives of the Proprietary Government. Their attitude toward dealing with such people was explained by Tiyanoga, a leading Mohawk chief to Sir William Johnson: "Men who are not brothers to the Indians ...and yet believe blindly what the Indians say - such men are fools and deserve whatever they receive." 18

Tiyonaga was a Mohawk and Guyasuta was a Seneca and both were leaders in the Iroquois Confederacy. We may rest assured that the words of Tiyonaga represented settled Iroquois policy. One had to be careful when dealing with them.

Another problem that we moderns have is the belief that the Indians with whom the settlers were most in contact - the Seneca, Delaware, and Shawnee - always lived here. We have been told so often that these people were here "for thousands of years" and that "they owned this land" that we begin to believe it. It is not true.

It is true that someone lived, or traveled through this area, in the distant past. Dr. James Aldovasio, an eminent archaeologist, has proven at the Meadowcroft Rock Shelter near Avella that some hunting groups were here 11,000 years ago. We know of the Mound-Builders in Moundsville, West Virginia, and other places, also of the Hopewell people. But these people were long gone by the 1700's. Instead, we have the Shawnee, Delaware, and Seneca - Iroquois. We know where they came from: the Seneca lived up around Erie, Pennsylvania and Buffalo, New York. On behalf of the Iroquois Confederacy they were the Keepers of the Western Door, the Iroquois tribes being spread out from Erie to Albany, New York where the Mohawks were the Keepers of the Eastern Door.

The Delaware lived, in historic times, along the Atlantic coast and adjacent to the Delaware River, around Philadelphia. When the Penns arrived the Delaware had never lived in Western Pennsylvania. They were gradually shoved westward because of land purchases by the State Government and by orders - in no uncertain terms - from the Iroquois.

We get back again to Indian politics and diplomacy. The Iroquois had conquered the Delaware and treated them like a subservient people. They told them where to live. When William Penn arrived he made the awful but innocent mistake of buying land from the Delaware, who occupied it. When the Iroquois found out about that they soon put a stop to it. Thereafter, the English discussed land purchases with the Iroquois, paid them, and the Iroquois not only told the Delaware to get out but told them where to live. And the Delaware moved - quickly!

Once the Delaware complained to the Quaker government that they had been cheated in one land sale - the famous Walking Purchase. The canny Quakers mentioned it to the Iroquois and brought about this diatribe by Canassatego, an Iroquois spokesman, to the Delaware chiefs:

"Cousins, let this Belt of Wampum serve to Chastise you. You ought to be taken by the Hair of your Head and shak'd severely till you recover your Senses and become Sober....We conquered you. We made women of you. You know you are women and can no more sell land than women...We charge you to remove instantly. We don't give you the liberty to think about it. You are women. Take the advice of a Wise Man and remove immediately...We therefor assign you two places to go, either Wyoming or Shamokin - you may go to either of these places and then we shall have you more under our Eye and shall see how you behave - Don't deliberate but remove away..."
19

That is tough talk - and the Delaware wisely "left town." Some moved up into the Wyoming Valley, near Scranton and Wilkes-Barre and others moved west along the Susquehanna River near Harrisburg. Years later that land would be sold and they would be told to live in Western Pennsylvania. Thus, instead of having lived here for generations, they were almost as new as the white settlers who followed them.

The conquest incident referred to by Canassatego appears to have occurred about 1710 when the Iroquois defeated the Delaware in battle and then humiliated them further by "putting petticoats" on them. A Shawnee Indian related the story:

"About a year after, the Five Nations told the Delawares and us, "since you have not hearkened to us nor regarded what we have said, now we will put petticoats on you, and look upon you as women for the future, and not as men." [20]

Needless to say, the Delaware seethed with resentment that all subjugated peoples do, but were powerless to stop the continuing insults.

The Shawnee were also newcomers to Western Pennsylvania, much like the white settlers. They were driven out of the Georgia-Florida area by the Cherokee and Catawba tribes, and slowly worked their way north-west, finally arriving in Illinois-Indiana. Then they turned East, now in historic times, and asked permission of the Iroquois to settle in Pennsylvania. This was granted and they moved close to the Delaware in the vicinity of the Delaware River. Thereafter their fate was dictated by the Iroquois and, by and large, their later movements roughly parallel that of the Delaware. In this area, when they finally got here, they settled in a few villages along the Allegheny River - Kittanning, Tarentum, and others - and eventually moved on west into Ohio when the white settlers began to arrive, and made their homes along the Scioto and Little Miami Rivers.

As you can see they are another group who arrived in Western Pennsylvania just one step before the white frontiersmen. So, it is simply not true - or a half-truth - to say that Indians lived here "for hundreds, thousand of years" before the coming of the white man. Someone was undoubtedly here, then disappeared, leaving no records and no stories. Neither the Iroquois, the Shawnee, nor the Delaware - the three dominate tribes in this area - have any traditions or folklore about other Indians being in Mt. Lebanon, Peters Township, Canonsburg, or Washington when they arrived.

There were other Indian tribes who habitually raided through this area and who did not own this land nor even pretend to any such claim. This was Iroquois country and they knew it and if they even hinted at any ownership rights the Iroquois would have come swooping down on them like an eagle on a rabbit.

These were the "western tribes," Chippewa, Ottawa, Wyandot, Pottawattomy, Illinois, and Kickapoo, to name some of the more prominent ones. And where did they live? They came from the areas of Toledo, Ohio, Detroit, Michigan, Chicago, Illinois, Milwaukee,

Wisconsin, Indianapolis, Indiana, and Louisville, Kentucky. They didn't own anything in Western Pennsylvania.

We might well ask - why were they raiding here? The simple answer is that this is what warriors did for a living. When they weren't raiding the white people they were fighting each other. To be sure they were encouraged in these raids first by the French and later by the English, and the promise of money for scalps and prisoners (which paid them handsomely by the way), but they didn't need much encouragement. Fighting was what warriors did - it was an ethic, a life-style.

A mention has been made that the Iroquois claimed ownership of this land and they sold it to the white people in 1768. Did that stop their raiding? Not at all. They continued their merciless assaults for another twenty-five years. Why? That's what warriors do. Naturally they found excuses for these attacks - the ingenuity of the human mind to justify its conduct is wonderful to behold, but in the end we come down to the warrior-ethic.

The Iroquois deserve special mention. They were in a class by themselves - the Nazi of Eastern United States in the 17th and 18th century. They controlled this country with an iron fist from the St. Lawrence River in the north to the Suwanee River in Georgia and from the Atlantic coast to the Mississippi River in the west. They were hard, tough, and cruel. They wiped out the Erie Indians at Erie, Pennsylvania (the Cat People) so completely that we only know of them by stories of nearby tribes. To almost the same extent they attacked and just decimated the Illinois in Illinois and the Huron Indians in Michigan. What fierce people! And masters of diplomacy.

When they went to war with another people it wasn't merely to conquer and dominate that tribe, their secondary motive was to wreak such havoc that word would spread to the four winds: " You, too, beware the power of the Iroquois." Everyone got the message - and heeded it!

"They came like foxes," wrote one chronicler, "attacked like lions, and fled like birds." 21 They drove the Huron from southern Canada, the Algonquin from northern Michigan, the Ottawa and Miami from southern Michigan and Ohio, subdued the Illinois tribe, and kept going until they reached the Mississippi. Oh, were they fierce! And, they treated the survivors with undisguised contempt.

Once, at a large council of several tribes, the Wyandots claimed the right to light the council fire - a very important and honored function. A Seneca chief, Red Jacket, disdainfully put an end to this claim:

"Have the (Wyandots) forgotten themselves? Or do they suppose we have forgotten them? Who gave you the right in the west or east, to light the general council fire? You must have fallen asleep, and dreamt that the Six Nations was dead! Who permitted you to escape from the lower country? Had you any heart left to speak a word for yourselves? Remember how you hung on by the bushes. You had not even a place to land on. You have not yet done pissing for fear of the (Iroquois)." 22

Minor raids - war party raids - for fun, fame, and fortune (plunder and prisoners) went on without let-up and were a constant reminder throughout eastern United States of the Iroquois presence. They actually had a well-worn warrior-path from Albany down to North Carolina and Georgia so that they could easily get there to raid the Catawba and Cherokee, favorite enemies. To put things in perspective, it is almost 1000 miles from Albany to Atlanta and another 1000 to get back home, and that was a routine raid for the Iroquois warriors. The Catawba and Cherokee weren't intimidated - they used the same trail heading north to New York!

The Iroquois League or Confederacy was formed about 1600 at the urging of the legendary Hiawatha who convinced the Seneca, Oneida, Mohawks, Cayauga, and Onondaga to stop killing each other and to get together. He succeeded and they were known as the Five Nations; in 1715 the Tuscaroras were permitted to join them and they became the Six Nations. They created a very advanced political structure for the time - way beyond anything that existed among other tribes.

Their homeland was in New York state from Albany in the east to Buffalo in the west, and extending to Erie, Pennsylvania. They were never large in number. All population figures are estimates, but it is pretty much agreed that they were about 20,000 people and they could, if they extended themselves, mobilize 3000 to 4000 warriors for a major effort.

They were nice people - among themselves and to their friends. A little haughty, quick to take offense, somewhat changeable in nature and, if not undependable exactly, they were quixotic. One salient quality - both as individuals and a tribe - is that they deliberated before they acted and thought out consequences. If you insulted an Iroquois today you wouldn't get into a fight - today. The man would contemplate the matter for a while - perhaps a long while. You were going to die, it was just a matter of when, where, and how he was going to kill you with the least consequences to himself.

They were a very smart people, adept at playing off one group of strangers or enemies against another. They played this game with the French, British, and Americans from the very first contact.

By our standards they were quite licentious, the girls began sexual activities at age 8 or 9, and the young women were the aggressors in sexual matters. 23 James Smith, the young man previously mentioned, was shocked at their behavior. He tells the story of three girls "ambushing" a young man to strip him of his clothes so they could determine "if he was yet a man." 24

At their very earliest meeting with white people they saw at once the superiority of woven clothes over fur skins, iron needles over bone ones, a musket over a bow, and an iron pot over the paunch of an animal. They also discovered rum - and loved it. They - along with all Indian tribes - became addicted to white man's goods and thus - more than anything else that happened - sowed the seeds of their own destruction. The addiction led to dependency on trade and the loss of old skills.

It is fun to look at the items the Indians got in 1742 when the Pennsylvania Proprietary government bought some land west of the Susquehanna River:

"...45 guns, lead and powder, 60 strowd matchcoats, 100 duffel matchcoats, 100 blankets, 60 kettles, 100 tobacco tongs, 120 combs, 2000 needles, 24 doz. garters, 40 hats, 40 pair of shoes, stockings and sundry other items." 25

Note the coats, garters, hats, shoes, stockings, and buckles. In the very earliest paintings of the Indians they are often shown, the men, wearing ruffled shirts and the women lovely dresses. These were the very latest fashion from London and Paris. It is rather hilarious to see these clothes in the wilderness, but we must remember that the clothes were made in England and France and, naturally, they were the fashionable clothes of the day.

Another amusing incident occurred at this transaction. The Indians looked over the items, looked into the faces of the representatives of the Proprietors, and sensed their eagerness to acquire the land and then spoke out:

"We ...desire, if you have the keys of the Proprietors Chest you will open it and take out a little more for us. We know our lands are now become more valuable...We are sensible that the Land is Everlasting and the few Goods we receive for it are soon worn out and gone..." 26

Those Six Nations bargainors were able to squeeze out another 300 British pounds worth of merchandise from the State - and that was a lot of money in those days.

How silly it is to read today about white people taking advantage of poor, ignorant savages. These people were traders from way back and knew how to drive a good bargain. They lived by the adage "Fool me once, shame on you; fool me twice, shame on me." They were never fooled twice.

In retrospect it may seem that they got the worst of the bargain, but don't forget that they were selling a piece of empty, forested land set in the middle of an endless expanse of equally empty forest land. Their view was that they had plenty more of what they were selling. What Arab would worry about selling 100 square miles of sand in the middle of the Sahara Desert! He might regret it, later, when oil was discovered under that sand, but at the time, he believed he was getting a good deal. It was much the same thing for an Indian in Pennsylvania in the 1700's.

Incidentally, the Iroquois League was an indirect casualty of the American Revolution. It self-destructed on October 20, 1775, during a Great Council when the Oneida and Tuscaroras decided to side with the Americans and the others opted for the British or neutrality. The council fire at Onondaga was extinguished, never again to be lit. It was all over.

The Indians
II. The Bad News

There were, however, three attributes of all of these Indians - Iroquois, Shawnee, and Delaware as well as the others - that did not sit well with white settlers, to-wit, on their raids against the settlements (and anywhere else) they were murderous brutes, killing toddlers running around in diapers and gray-haired Grandmas as quickly as they would an armed man. Secondly, they engaged in the most hideous tortures imaginable (they loved it, they reveled in it, it was their Saturday Night Entertainment); and finally, they were cannibals.

This caused problems, what we now call "irreconcilable differences."

The white settlers understood fighting and they understood war, but they weren't quite willing to accept a grown man, a warrior, picking up a baby by its feet and smashing its head against a convenient tree or stone, then going out into a yard and chasing down terrified, screaming little kids, burying his tomahawk in their heads or cutting their throats, then scalping them.

That really wasn't acceptable behavior to the settlers. They objected. They went insane with fury. One minister spoke for all, when he said of his parishioners, "What could I do with men heated to madness? All that I could do was done; I expostulated; but life and reason were set at defiance..." 27

In acting in this manner the Indians weren't picking on white people, this was how they behaved on raids. They didn't discriminate against anyone, they treated all enemies (anyone they disliked), equally barbarously and expected, if defeated, that they, their women and children, would be treated in the same way.

All white people were shocked at this conduct. The Earl of Chatham, Edmond Burke, in a speech to the Parliament called them "the Horrible hell-hounds of savage war." 28 A French officer, Louis Bougainville, said of them: "What a scourge! Humanity shudders at being obliged to make use of such monsters." 29 George Washington wrote about the Indian raids on the frontiers people: "Every day we have accounts of such cruelties and barbarities as are shocking to human nature." 30 Washington had been around long enough, and had seen enough fighting, that it took a lot to shock him. A Governor of Pennsylvania referred to the "barbarous Indians, who delight in shedding human blood, and who make no distinction as to age or sex...; all are alike the objects of their cruelty - slaughtering the tender infant, and frightened mother, with equal joy and fierceness." 31

The Corbly Family Massacre Site

This memorial is on the east side of the village of Garard's Fort, adjacent to the Garard Fort Cemetery. The Indians hid in the gully which runs from left to right in the background. The family came from over the hill in the rear, beyond the gully.

A close up of the monument.

This shows the hill down which the family strolled that beautiful morning. The gully runs from left to right at the bottom of this picture. Garard's Fort, toward which they were headed, was about 700 yards away.

Thomas Jefferson who grew up on the frontiers of western Virginia even put this explicit comment into our Declaration of Independence when he mentioned:

"...the merciless Indian Savages, whose known rule of warfare, is an undistinguished destruction of all ages, sexes and conditions."

One has to reflect on the vehemence of these expressions: "hell-hounds," "barbarous," "merciless savages," "cruel and barbaric," "monsters," - they were very well justified. The Indians worked hard to earn these curses.

It is worthwhile to mention just a few stories of hundreds that could be told. These are not novel or unique examples but perfectly routine, everyday types of events that happened here in western Pennsylvania in Olden Times.

The Rev. Corbly was walking with his family to his church one beautiful May morning. While he thought about his sermon his wife and five children got a little ahead of him. Suddenly a small party of Indians struck. They shot and tomahawked Mrs. Corbly. A baby she was carrying lay beside her, its brains splattered on a nearby tree and it was scalped. Little Mary Ann, aged two, and Katherine, aged 4, were killed and scalped. Isaiah, a 6 year old, was badly wounded and scalped. He died the next day. Elizabeth and Delilah were older girls and both were wounded and scalped. Delilah never recovered from her wounds, and this horrible ordeal, and died a few years later. Elizabeth did recover. The Rev. Corbly was chased by an Indian with whom he grappled and finally broke away and ran for help to a nearby fort.

Margaret, the oldest girl, was already at the fort (in which services were to be held) and she describes the scene when her family was brought in:

"...her mother...dangling across the withers of a horse, the skirt of the dress which was a black silk one, had been cut off close to the waist, and she was frightfully mangled and smeared with gore, presenting a spectacle more ghastly than language can portray."

The little boy "...Isaiah, lived twenty-four hours and revived enough to cry deliriously for the Indians to spare his life..."

The Reverend observed his wife's struggle: "My wife had a suckling baby in her arms; this little infant they killed and scalped. They then struck my wife several times, but not getting her down. The Indian who aimed to shoot me ran to her, shot her through her body and scalped her." 32

This was typical Indian warfare; a perfectly routine incident.

Mary Jemison (previously mentioned) at age 13 was captured by some Shawnee along with her mother and father, her little brothers Robert and Matthew, and sister Betsy. A neighbor woman who was visiting and her two children were also captured. She tells us that "on our march that day, an Indian went behind us with a whip, with which he frequently lashed the children, to make them keep up." She adds, "Whenever the little children cried for water, the Indians would make them drink urine, or go thirsty." At one point Mary and one of the neighbor's little boys were separated from the others and marched ahead some distance. A little later the Indians who had stayed behind appeared but without the other prisoners. That night Mary had to watch while the Indians pulled some scalps from their bags and began to scrape them, dry them, attach them to hoops they had made, and then carefully comb the hair. "Those scalps I knew at the time must have been taken from my family, by the color of the hair. My mother's hair was red; and I could easily distinguish my father's and the children's from each other. The sight was most appalling...." 33

It is difficult for us to even imagine such a scene and the effect it would have on a thirteen year old girl.

She was later told that the remains of her family had been found "mangled in the most shocking manner."

Similar stories are endless.

William Crawford (who was later to be tortured and burned to death by Indians) wrote from Pittsburgh about conditions in this area. It was a routine report:

"On the 6th and 7th instant, they killed and scalped one man at Raccoon Creek, about twenty five miles from this place; at Muchmore's plantation, about forty five miles down the Ohio, they killed and scalped one man, and burnt a woman and her four children; at Wheeling they killed and scalped one man, the body of whom was much mangled with tomahawks...; at Dunkards Creek...they killed and scalped one man and a woman and took three children...." 34

One could go on and on with a hundred and one such reports.

Another aspect of Indian nature that was abhorrent to the white settlers was their love of torture. The Indians seemed to revel in it and "stayed up nights" devising new ways to make their prisoners suffer. When several prisoners were captured the war party would drop off one or two at each village through which it passed on the way home for the purpose of torture.

Mary Jemison describes her observations at a Shawnee town:

"On the way we passed a Shawnee town, where I saw a number of heads, arms, legs, and other fragments of the bodies of some white people who had just been burned. The parts that remained were hanging on a pole, which was supported at each end by a crotch stuck in the ground, and were roasted or burnt black as a coal. The fire was yet burning; and the whole appearance afforded a spectacle so shocking that even to this day the blood almost curdles in my veins when I think of them." 35

She was traded to the Senecas and spent the rest of her life with them. She describes her second husband, Hickatoo, and his ability at torture in these words:

"In early life he showed signs of thirst for blood...and in practicing cruelties upon everything that chanced to fall into his hands which was susceptible of pain...

He could inflict the most excruciating tortures upon his enemies, and prided himself upon his fortitude having performed the most barbarous ceremonies and tortures without the least degree of pity or remorse." 36

This man was clearly a monster but Mary tells us he was a nice person at home. She had several children by him. He became a leader of the Seneca and led many of their raids against the frontier settlements and undoubtedly practiced his tortures on white men, women, and children who fell into his hands.

The stories of the tortures inflicted by these Indians are as numerous as the stories of their killing women and children and for the same reason - it was so common. These stories are ugly in their details, but they represent a reality that the settlers had to live with, and reading of them can help us appreciate some of the horror of frontier life.

Only three such stores will be related here - the well-know death of Col. Crawford, the killing of a poor, unknown white woman, and the torture of John Turner. I might tell of Lt. Boyd but his death was so horrible it even shocked the hardened frontiersmen, so we will leave it.

The death of Col. Crawford was witnessed by Dr. Knight (who was told the same thing would be done to him the next day). Knight tells us:

"In a few minutes a large stake was fixed in the ground...Col. Crawford's hands were then tied behind his back; a strong rope was produced, one end of which was fastened to the ligature, between his wrists, and the other tied to the bottom of the stake. The rope was long enough to permit him to walk around the stake several times and then return.

****

His ears had been cut off and the blood was streaming down his face.

****

The Warriors shot charges of powder into his naked body, commencing with the calves of his legs, and continuing to his neck. The boys snatched...burning hickory poles and applied them to his flesh. As fast as he ran around the stake to avoid one party of tormentors, he was promptly met at every turn by others with burning poles, red-hot irons, and rifles loaded with powder only; so that in a few minutes nearly one hundred charges of powder had been shot into his body, which had become black and blistered in a dreadful manner. The squaws would rake up a quantity of coals and hot ashes, and throw them upon his body, so that in a few minutes, he had nothing but fire to walk upon.

****

The terrible scene had now lasted more than two hours, and Crawford had become much exhausted.

****

At length he sunk in a fainting fit upon his face, and lay motionless. Instantly an Indian sprung upon his back...made a circular incision with his knife upon the crown of his head, and, clapping the knife between his teeth, tore the scalp off with both hands. Scarcely had this been done, when a withered hag approached with a board full of burning embers, and poured them upon the crown of his head, now laid bare to the bone. The Colonel groaned deeply, arose and again walked slowly around the stake - But why continue a description so horrible. Nature, at length, could endure no more, and at a late hour in the night, he was released by death, from the hands of his tormentors." 37

(Dr. Knight had seen all that he wanted to see - the next day he escaped.)

Participating in this torture were 30 warriors and about 60 women and boys. As you can see it was a community affair. In the villages torture was always a community affair. Mary Jemison tells us that "it was one of the highest kinds of frolics ever celebrated in their tribe." 38

That this was a long-standing practice is obvious from a story told by Francis Parkman about the torture of some Algonquin Indians - both men and women - at an Iroquois village. This was in 1641 and he writes:

"On the following morning, they (the prisoners) were placed on a large scaffold, in sight of the whole population. It was a gala-day. Young and old were gathered from far and near. Some mounted the scaffold, and scorched them with torches and firebrands; while the children standing beneath the bark platform, applied fire to the feet of the prisoners between the crevices." 39

At Kittanning two captured white women - Marie Le Roy and Barbara Leninger were forced to watch the torture of some unknown white woman who had tried to escape and was recaptured:

"First, they scalped her; next they laid burning splinters of wood, here and there, upon her body; and then they cut off her ears and fingers, forcing them into her mouth so that she had to swallow them. Amidst such torments this woman lived from nine o'clock in the morning until toward sunset...When she was dead, the Indians chopped her in two, through the middle, and let her lie until the dogs came and devoured her." 40

As a matter of fact, a French soldier traveling with the Indians couldn't stand it any longer and shot the woman in the head to put her out of her misery. In so doing that French soldier risked his own life. The Indians didn't tolerate this kind of interference in their ways - torture or otherwise. Most likely the woman had stopped screaming, the Indians were now bored with the whole thing, and the Frenchman saw a chance to end this melancholy affair.

Another such hideous death is that of John Turner who was tortured in front of his wife and children. This also happened at Kittanning by Delawares. First several warriors heated their musket barrels red-hot in a fire and rammed them into his body. A woman sliced off his ears and ate them. Then some men cut off his fingers, penis, and testicles. Following this his scalp was torn off. All of this was done in a leisurely manner to the laughter and approving cries of the crowd. Turner was still not dead so a six year old boy was given a tomahawk and lifted up by his father so that he could pound on Turner's skull, finally caving it in. At last John Turner died. 41

We are told that:

A common torture of the Iroquois Indians was to prepare a great quantity of wooden splinters about the thickness of a pencil at one end and tapering to a sharp point at the other, each about five inches long. These would be soaked in turpentine or pitch and them stuck into the naked body of a bound captive at random until he might take on the appearance of a pincushion. The pain of the turpentine or pitch in the wounds alone was excruciating, but these splinters would than be set afire. Some victims would be able to remain alive in such condition for three hours or more." 42

Enough of this. Suffice it to say that these tortures were routine in Indian life and they were all bad. They did nothing to encourage good relations between the Indians and the white settlers. They inspired the flames of hatred by the white people and kept the fires roaring.

Finally, the third aspect of Indian life that made the white people very uncomfortable was the cannibalism.

Everyone who came into contact with the woodland Indians observed it, commented about it, and hated it.

The Indians ate human flesh for two reasons: one, they were hungry; secondly, if the man had been a brave enemy, they thought that by eating some portion of his body they would gain his fighting spirit and strength.

The great historian, Francis Parkman, mentions this trait in his classic, The Jesuits in North America, several times, and also in Montcalm and Wolfe, Part I, including this story: "At the first halt, the captors (Iroquois) took the infants from their mothers, tied them to wooden spits, placed them to die slowly before a fire, and feasted upon them before the eyes of the agonized mothers..." 43

Capt. Pouchot, who was long in North America and was the French commander at Ft. Niagara, mentions it as do many other observer-authors. Allan Eckert, the great author about colonial days, and one who has an encyclopedic knowledge of the Indians tells story after story in his books, principally, Wilderness Empire, that some Miami Indians killed ten French traders and ate them; that Pontiac, the great Ottawa chief, cut out the heart of a Indian trader and ate it, and a group of his followers boiled and ate the bodies of three enemy Indians and a trader. 44 After Braddock's defeat here at Pittsburgh, some Ottawas captured Mary Francis and five other women along with seven men. On the way to their villages the Indians became quite hungry and proceeded to dismember Mary Francis and two of the men and boiled and ate them. The gruesome details are given in Wilderness Empire 51 for those who are interested.

Louis Bougainville was a French officer during the French & Indian War, and he was an astute observer of his Indian allies. He hated them. He cites instance after instance of their eating prisoners: "They put in the pot and ate three prisoners...A horrible spectacle to European eyes," 45 "...they ate one of them up at this camp. It is impossible to stop them," 46 "An English corpse came floating by the Indian's camp. They crowded around it with loud cries, drank its blood, and put its pieces in the kettle." 47

Our local Indians shared in these activities. Bougainvile goes on, "The Delewares and Shawnees have made many prisoners....They have eaten an English officer whose pallor and plumpness tempted them. Such cruelties are frequent enough among the Indians of La Belle Riviere." 48

The river he speaks of is the Allegheny and the Ohio - the French thought of them as one river and called it the Beautiful River. The river may have been lovely, but one cannot say the same for the Indians who lived on it.

Numerous other sources and stories could be cited but it becomes redundant.

This cannibalism did not habitually occur in their own villages except in times of famine. The Indians preferred deer, bear, and other wild game. It usually happened when they were far from home, in unfamiliar county, and had to camp for many days for some good reason. Cannibalism was also utilized when they were coming back from a raid, were in a hurry, and had several hundred miles to travel. In this circumstance they had no time to hunt and a prisoner provided a convenient source of food. 49

It happened and it was bad.

Any one of these Indian characteristics - the merciless killing of defenseless woman and children, the tortures, or the cannibalism - would have been enough to fill the white settlers with an enormous hatred of the Indians. Since the frontierspeople had to contend with all three it was too much. Perhaps it was at this time there developed the old adage that "the only good Indian is a dead Indian."

Before leaving this short review of the Indians one might satisfy an inquiring mind who asks: "If the settlers were so filled with rage, why didn't they go after the Indians? There are several answers to this query:

1. The settlers were farmers, not soldiers; the Indians were warriors, not farmers. That was a vast difference. In most of the small-scale battles on the frontier the Indians won because they were trained, experienced fighters and the settlers were not. The frontierspeople performed adequately in defensive fighting from their little settlers forts and in guerrilla warfare around their settlements, but they couldn't often mount successful large scale raids against Indian villages.

2. The Indian villages were from fifty to two or three hundred miles away from the scenes of their attacks. No group of settlers could leave their farms for the time it would take to march to a village, say, near Chicago, Illinois or Albany, New York. In addition those Indians would know an army was coming when it was miles away. Then, they would either set up an ambush or gather their families and fade away into the forest. If the settlers got there at all there would be no one to fight. This was a common Indian tactic.

3. The settlers rarely got help from anyone - not the Quaker government in Philadelphia, nor the Crown in London, nor the Continental Congress. They lacked men,

guns, powder, lead, money, training, and time. Thus they had little chance in a long distance raid against these Indians.

In general, it can be said that all the settlers could do was to cry, curse, and fight back from their homes or forts.

But they didn't leave.

NOTES

Three: THE INDIANS

1. James Smith, *Scoouwa: James Smith's Indian Captivity Narrative* (Columbus, Ohio: Ohio Historical Society, 1978), p.62.
2. Ibid., p. 60.
3. Pierre Pouchot, *Memoirs On the Late War In North America Between France and England, Ed. By Brian Leigh Dunnigan* (Youngstown, New York: Old Fort Niagara Association, Inc., 1994), p. 474.
4. Edward P. Hamilton, ed., *Adventure In the Wilderness: The American Journals of Louis Antoine Bougainville 1756 - 1760* (Norman, Okla.: Univ. Of Oklahoma Press, 1964), p. 103-104.
5. James E. Seaver, *The Life of Mary Jemison* (Jersey Shore, Pa., Zebrowski Historical Service & Pub. Co., 1991), p. 141.
    This is a reprint of the Fifth Edition.
6. Ibid., p. 18.
7. Ibid., p. 70.
8. Ibid., p. 72.
9. Ibid., p. 73.
10. Ibid., p. 67.
11. Smith, p. 90.
12. Henry R. Schoolcraft, *Notes On The Iroquois* (Germantown, N.Y.: Periodical Service, Inc., 1975), p. 298.
    This is a reprint of the original published in 1847.
13. I.D. Rupp, *Early History of Western Pennsylvania* (Lewisburg, PA: Wennawoods Publishing, 1995; originally published, 1846, Harrisburg, Pa.), p. 172.
14. Ibid., Appendix XVI, p. 151.
15. Ibid., Appendix X, p. 91.
16. Ibid., Appendix XIX, p. 188.
17. Allan W. Eckert, *That Dark and Bloody River* (New York, NY: Bantam Books, 1995), p. 672 f.n. 252.
18. Allan W. Eckert, *Wilderness Empire* (Boston, Mass.: Little, Brown and Company, 1969), p. 83.
    Eckert relies on historical data, but to make his history books more interesting, he deliberately creates conversations. He insists the facts are accurate and that this technique is employed only to make history "come alive."
19. Joseph J. Kelley, Jr., *Pennsylvania: The Colonial Years, 1681-1776* (Garden City, NY: Doubleday & Company, Inc., 1980), p. 224.
20. C. Hale Sipe, *The Indian Chiefs of Pennsylvania* (Lewisburg, Pa.: Wennawoods Publishing, 1994), p. 111.
    This is a reprint of the original published in 1927.
21. Ray Allen Billington, *Westward Expansion* (New York, NY: The Macmillan Company, 1967), p. 104.
22. Schoolcraft, p. 424.
23. Pouchot, p. 446.
24. Smith, p. 86.
25. Kelly, 223.
26. Ibid.
27. Ibid., p. 491.
28. Lewis S. Shimmell, *Border Warfare In Pennsylvania* (Harrisburg, Pa.: R.L. Myers & Company, 1901), p. 37.

29. Hamilton, ed., *Bougainville*, p. 191
30. Francis Parkman, *France and England In North America, Vol. VIII Montcalm and Wolfe, Part I* (New York, N.Y.: Frederick Ungar Publishing Co., 1965), p. 331. This is a reprint of the 1884 edition.
31. Rupp, p. 118.
32. Earle R. Forrest, *History of Washington County, Pennsylvania*(Chicago, Ill.: S.J. Clarke Publishing Company, 1926), p. 161; Rupp, Appendix XXXII, p. 338,
33. Seaver, *Mary Jemison*, pp. 43-49.
34. Reuben Gold Thwaites and Louise Phelps Kellogg, Ed's, *The Revolution On The Upper Ohio, 1775-1777* (Port Washington, N.Y.: Kennikat Press, 1908), pp. 250-251.
35. Seaver, *Mary Jemison, p.* 56.
36. Ibid., pp. 185-186.
37. Rupp, pp. 214-215.
38. Seaver, *Mary Jemison,* p. 99.
39. Francis Parkman, *The Jesuits In North America* (Williamstown, Mass.: Corner House Publishers, 1980), p. 345; originally published in 1867.
40. John W. Harpster, ed., *Pen Pictures of Early Western Pennsylvania* (Univ. Of Pittsburgh Press, 1938), pp. 54-55.
41. Eckert, *Wilderness Empire*, pp. 406-407.
42. Allan W. Eckert, *Wilderness War* (Boston, Mass.: Little, Brown and Company, 1978), p. 452, f.n. 137.
43. Parkman, *Jesuits*, p. 343.
44. Eckert, *Wilderness Empire*, pp. 183, 185, 188, 189.
45. Hamilton, ed., *Bougainville*, p. 143.
46. Ibid., p. 146.
47. Ibid., p. 150.
48. Ibid., p. 114.
49. Eckert, *Wilderness War*, p. 452, f.n. 141.

Chapter 4
The Rangers

Someone had to go looking for Indians prowling around the neighborhood. It didn't do to have a fort to run to but nobody to tell you when to run. Doddridge tells us of an "express" arriving in the dead of night with a report that the Indians were at hand. "The express came softy to the door, or back window, and by a gently tapping waked the family." Who was the "express?" He was a neighbor, on temporary duty with the local militia group.

Of necessity every man belonged to the militia and each unit was identified either by the neighborhood, i.e. the Peters Creek Rangers, or by the name of the commander, i.e., Brady's Rangers. These people would always be called together in an emergency but it was in the area of routine patrolling, when Indians were not known to be around, that problems arose. Obviously a man could not farm and be on patrol at the same time. The solution to this problem was to call up a few men continuously for only short periods of time, one month and two month tours of duty are most often mentioned. During crucial parts of the farming season such as the planting and harvesting periods the young boys and old men would serve in place of those husky persons who had to be out working in the fields. Thus Eliel Long tells us that in September, 1778, he was "out" for two months and that "he next went out in May, 1779, under Capt. John Minor for two months; in 1780 he served for one month under Captain Rail."

Harrod Newland was only thirteen years old in March, 1779, when he went out with Capt. Jesse Pigman to pursue a party of Indians and:

"After about four or five days of ranging, he returned to his own neighborhood with his party, and finding all the inhabitants now forted at different stations and blockhouses, he was at this time engaged in spying until the last of October, when his company was dismissed and sent home, since their object was not to make long marches or carry off offensive warfare, but merely to guard and defend the frontier and warn the inhabitants of danger while they carried on their agricultural pursuits."

James Pribble was only fifteen years old and in March, 1777, he served for six months and his duty was "to guard the Fort and range the line of settlements to prevent the Indians...from raiding the frontier country." 1

These men were the "express" to which Rev. Doddridge refers in his book.

For their service these men were paid (sometimes) by the government, whoever that might be, now the Royal Governor or the Quaker Assembly in Philadelphia, later the State of

Pennsylvania or the new Federal government. No matter what, or who, it was, "government" was always short of money and hated to spend it for military purposes. This caused serious problems and resentments among the frontier people. As an example of their reaction in desperate times consider this letter from Arthur St. Clair to Governor Penn dated May 29, 1774:

"Sir:

The panic that has struck this country, threatening an entire depopulation thereof, induced me a few days ago to make an excursion to Pittsburgh, to see if it can be removed and the desertion prevented.

The only probable remedy that offered was to afford the people the appearance of some protection. Accordingly, Mr. Smith, Mr. Mackay, Mr. Butler, and some others of the inhabitants of Pittsburgh, with Col. Croghan and myself, entered into an association for the immediate raising of an hundred men, to be employed as a ranging company, to cover the inhabitants in case of danger, to which association several of the magistrates and other inhabitants have acceded and in a very few days they will be on foot.

We have undertaken to maintain them for one month, at the rate of one shilling and six pence a man per diem; this we will cheerfully discharge, at the same time we flatter ourselves that your Honor will approve the measure, and that the Government will not only relieve private persons from the burthen but take effectual measures for the safety of this frontier, and this I am desired by the people in general to request of your Honor. I am Sir, your most obedient, most humble servant,

Arthur St. Clair" 2

We are left to wonder whether these public-spirited citizens were ever repaid!

The citizen-militia were certainly an essential part of the defense of the frontiers, but it wasn't enough. Someone was needed to engage in long-range "spying trips" deep into Indian country and to actively seek out and engage incoming war-parties and do all of this on a permanent basis. This could not be men who were trying to be farmers one day and had to be militia the next. Something more was required.

This need brought about the creation of specialized Ranger units who were on the government payroll and served for an extended period of time. They were formed into small units of highly skilled, audacious men and sent out to patrol extensively along the rivers and throughout the countryside looking for signs of Indian war-parties. They were also expected to go on spying missions to the Indian villages as far as two hundred miles away.

The idea was an old and sound one. Perhaps everyone will recall the stories about Roger's Rangers who operated in upper New York and Vermont; in central Pennsylvania Smith and his Black Boys did the same thing. In the Pittsburgh area and all of Western Pennsylvania Brady's Rangers was the elite unit. Commanded by Samuel Brady this unit, never large in number, was highly effective. 3

These Rangers had certain things in common beginning with a deep hatred of Indians. Every man had lost children, parents, wives, brothers, or sisters to Indian raiders. Sam Brady had experienced this loss - his brother and father had been killed by Indians and he took an oath to fight them until they were all dead, or he was dead, or he had driven them to their knees. This was no idle matter; it was not a man "shooting off his mouth," he meant it and he wanted men around him who felt the same way.

Secondly, all of these men were born and reared on this frontier, grew up intimately acquainted with the rivers and forests, and knew every skill for survival in this harsh environment. No recent immigrants need apply! They were expert shots with a rifle, could throw a tomahawk accurately, were physically strong, and possessed of extraordinary stamina.

Finally, each man had a well-established reputation for courage and audacity.

They were quite a crew.

Sam Brady trained them to do things his way. He showed them how to set up an ambush; to use intricate hand signals instead of speaking or calling out to one another; he honed their skills in following the dimmest trail of a war-party; and he taught them Indians tactics, those which they might expect to encounter and which they might themselves use.

He dressed them as Indians. George Raush was one of them, and he describes their appearance:

"...he was then stationed at Ft. Pitt (in 1775)...In obedience to the order of his...Captain Brady, he proceeded to tan his thighs and legs with wild cherry and white oak bark and to equip himself after the following manner, to-wit, a breechcloth, leather leggings, moccasins and a cap made out of a raccoon skin, with the feathers of a hawk, painted after the manner of an Indian warrior. His face was painted red, with three black stripes across his cheeks, which was a signification of war. Declarant states that Capt. Brady's company was about sixty-four in number, all painted after the manner aforesaid." 4

These Rangers had four specific jobs:

1. To patrol the rivers and creeks. All of the land west of the Allegheny River and both north and west of the Ohio was Indian country. War-parties had to cross these rivers to get to the settlements and they often left tell-tale signs when they did so, signs that sharp eyes could see and decipher. This was extremely hazardous work since it involved a few men in a canoe, openly exposed, paddling slowly along the river studying its banks for Indian "sign" - that tell-tale scraping of the mud to indicate a canoe dragged ashore, blackened pieces of wood and gray ashes to mark a camp fire, a dim path through the underbrush or the breaking of branches that would indicate movement of a body of Indians. Little things had meaning to experienced eyes. When "sign" was discovered the Rangers had the duty to begin spreading the word among the settlers.

2. When the presence of war-parties was discovered the Rangers would deliberately seek them out to destroy them or drive them away.

3. If raids had already taken place and prisoners were taken they would try to find the trail, follow it, and re-capture the prisoners.

4. When intelligence was received that the Indians were holding councils at their villages in preparation for raids the Rangers would travel long distances to these villages and there, hidden in the woods for several days, they would observe whether war-parties were being formed and where they were planning to go. This was certainly the most dangerous and daunting experience that anyone could be asked to do. Heaven help the Ranger who was caught - he faced hideous torture and death.

It took a special breed of men to do this work and they suffered a lot of casualties.

Usually Brady had about fifty men available to him. Their patrols were of the two man, four man, variety and a scouting unit never exceeded twenty-four men. If a specific, large scale attack was called for everyone would be utilized.

Some men who acquired fame as Rangers, in addition to Brady, are Lewis Wetzel, Andrew Poe, Tom Eddington, Sam Murphy, and Simon Kenton. They were legends in their own time and the stories of their exploits can still bring gasps of amazement.

An example of the Rangers at work is a story about Brady and two of his men who were patrolling along the Ohio River just a few miles from Pittsburgh and near present day Sewickley. They picked up an Indian trial and followed it as it headed toward the cabin of Albert Gray and his family. Shortly thereafter Gray, who had been out hunting, came ambling along. When he saw the Rangers, the trail, and the direction it was headed he immediately became a passionate participant in this scout. In due course they came upon his cabin, a smoldering ruins of burnt logs and ashes. There was no trace of Mrs. Gray nor the two children so it was obvious that they had been taken prisoner and were probably still alive, for the moment at least. The men moved on, anxious and worried now but very cautious, and after several more miles and near dusk they discovered twelve Indians camped in a ravine eating their supper. Mrs. Gray and the children were with them. The Rangers were hopelessly out-numbered so they gave no thought to an immediate attack. Instead they hid themselves in the woods surrounding the ravine and waited.

We are left to speculate about the feelings of Albert Gray as he lay there watching his family - so near and yet so far - and worrying that the Indians might elect to kill them rather than continue on with them as prisoners. Prisoners slowed down a war-party and at the least suspicion that they were being followed the Indians killed them. The British paid a fair price for scalps including those of women and children.

Eventually the Indians went to sleep and in the deepest, darkest hours of the night the three Rangers and Albert Gray crept forward and into the camp. Four rifle shots rang out and then the men resorted to tomahawk and knife to kill some of the remaining Indians. A startled few managed to run away into the woods.

The Gray family was saved. 5

Undoubtedly they went back to their land, re-built their home and commenced living again. We have to wonder, how did these people take these terrible ordeals and keep coming back? What extraordinary people! When settled into their new cabin the Grays knew there would be other Indian raids, perhaps tomorrow, perhaps next year, but they would come. The settlers in this region lived with this horrible chaos all of their lives - fighting and killing, blood and tears.

But they wouldn't leave.

Another Ranger tale is the occasion when a large war-party of Mingos, Senecas, and Wyandots were raising havoc in this area. Brady, hearing the reports, decided that a sizable response was needed so he gathered forty of his men and lit out after the raiders. He followed their trail from Pittsburgh all the way to Kent, Ohio - about one hundred and twenty miles - and there he found the Indians he was after. There were about sixty warriors in the camp. The Rangers had no hesitancy about instigating a fight. Sam elected to use an old Indian trick - he set up an ambush with twenty-eight of his Rangers and boldly approached the Indians camp with the twelve remaining men. They managed to get within sixty yards of the Indians and fired, killing several of them, and creating consternation amongst the rest. The Rangers immediately turned on their heels and ran like fury, the angry warriors right behind them. It worked beautifully. Brady and his men led the Indians directly between the lines of the hidden Rangers where they were quickly shot down. Any survivors of the rifle fire were attacked by men wielding tomahawks and that quickly ended the affray. Then it was the turn of the Rangers to "quietly and swiftly fade away into the forest." 6

The stories of these men are legion, and all of them awe-inspiring. Their skill and nerve places them in a class by themselves. They were special.

General Hand, in Pittsburgh, wrote a report on November 2, 1777, in which he, very laconically, discusses another long-range patrol deep into Indian country:

"Tom Nichols and party are returned; they were out six weeks and one day; he had been at Muncey and Musquaghty towns (on the Allegheny), Le Boeuf (Waterford, PA, near Erie) and to the head of French Creek, but could not discover any appearance of a regular enemy." 7

What nerve! For forty-three days, Tom Nichols "and party" were gone, their lives at risk every day, as they hiked along the Allegheny River. At the Delaware villages they would hide in the underbrush and watch the activities then move on. Further up the Allegheny they would spy out the Seneca villages, then turn left into French Creek (at present Franklin, PA) and proceed along its banks, past the village of the very dangerous Guyasuta, and on to Le Boeuf (at Waterford). Every day would have its hazards. How did they possibly avoid women working in corn fields, men going hunting, visitors passing to and from the several villages, canoes on the rivers, children at play, barking dogs? They had to stay near each village long enough to study the activities of the men and to watch for the gathering, or leaving, of war parties. At the end of this mission, with the intelligence gathered, they had to travel over a hundred miles, avoiding hunters or returning war-parties, to get back to Pittsburgh.

Just a routine patrol.

Thank you, Tom Nichols.

Finally, as an example of a local militia group at work and the problems they faced let us re-live the story of Andrew Poe and a Wyandot warrior named Dakadulah. 8

A war-party of seven Indians was raiding in the Fall of 1781, September to be exact, and they attacked the cabin of Philip Jackson, took him prisoner and plundered the place. Shortly after they left young Billy Jackson came home, saw the cabin in a state of disarray, his father missing, and he guessed what had happened. He ran for help and soon came across Andrew Poe, a neighbor, and explained the situation to him. Poe commanded the local militia and he happened to have twelve men at hand at Cherry's Fort. They started at once picking up the trail at the Jackson cabin. They followed the war-party for a day and a half and then, along the banks of the Ohio River, they discovered their quarry. Mr. Jackson was bound and sitting along the bank while the warriors were busy building two rafts to get them across the river. The militia men crept stealthily forward then, suddenly, one of them made a noise. The Indians were instantly alert, stopped their work and grabbed their rifles.

Andrew Poe has worked his way through the weeds to the top of an embankment. Below him were two warriors, one of them a very large man we now know was named Dakadulah. Poe aimed his rifle at the larger man - and it misfired. The click of the hammer in that tense moment might as well have been the roar of a cannon because both Indians heard it and immediately raised their rifles toward Poe. Andrew threw his rifle aside and leapt down on the two men below. He knocked Dakadulah down and wrapped his left arm around his neck then desperately reached out with his right hand and grasped the other Indian by the throat. A terrible struggle began as both Indians fought to get free, rolling and twisting, grasping Poe's arms to shake loose. Andrew didn't dare release his grip to reach for either his knife or tomahawk, but he couldn't hang on forever against these struggling men. Finally the smaller Indian broke loose and pulling his tomahawk began to slash at Poe and succeeded in striking his left arm leaving a seven inch gash. The pain and numbness that followed forced Poe to release his grip on Dakadulah who immediately ran into the river.

In the meantime Adam Poe, Andrew's brother, arrived on the scene and shot the smaller Indian in the chest, killing him.

Andrew ran into the water after Dakadulah and the two men fought and wrestled in the knee-deep water, churning its surface into a muddy froth. At this point the shore-line dropped off quickly and the two men soon found themselves in deep water and it was a fight to the death. Each man tried to grasp the head of the other and shove it under water and first one went down then the other.

By this time, all of the Indians on shore were dead, Billy Jackson stood by his father, and the other militia men gathered on the shore and watched the deadly struggle in the river.

The two fighters rose and sank, rolling, twisting, splashing, the battle going on underwater as much as above it. One head would rise gasping for air then sink again and the other head would suddenly appear to take in a breath. At last Andrew's head and shoulder appeared, both arms still deep in the water. Then he was seen to relax, turn and start to swim to shore. Dakadulah never came to the surface.

One of the white men had been led some distance away by the Indian he was tracking and, after killing that warrior, he was late in joining his friends. As he ran along the shore toward them he mistook Andrew for an Indian swimming in the river and fired, the rifle-ball striking Andrew in the right shoulder.

Wounded and exhausted Andrew Poe made it to shore - and collapsed. It would take days for him to recover his strength and weeks for the wounds to heal.

It was a tough life.

NOTES

Four: THE RANGERS

1. Howard Leckey, *The Ten Mile Country and Its Pioneer Families* (Knightstown, Ind.: Green County Historical Society, 1977), pp. 20-21.
2. Neville B. Craig, ed., *The Olden Time, Vol. I* (Pittsburgh, Pa.: Dumars & Co., 1846), p. 498; this was reprinted in 1876 by Robert Clarke & Co., Cincinnati, Ohio.
3. Allan W. Eckert, *That Dark and Bloody River* (New York, NY: Bantam Books, 1995), p. 293.
4. Richard B. La Crosse, Jr., *The Frontier Rifleman* (Union City, Tenn.: Pioneer Press, 1989), p. 70-71.
5. C. Hale Sipe, *Fort Ligonier and Its Times* (Arno Press & The New York Times, 1971), p. 475.
6. Eckert, *Dark and Bloody River*, pp. 293-296.
7. Reuben Gold Thwaites and Louise Phelps Kellogg, Ed's, *Frontier Defense On The Upper Ohio, 1777-1778* (Madison, Wis.: Wisconsin Historical Society, 1912), p. 147.
8. Eckert, *Dark and Bloody River*, pp. 285-288.
   This is another of the very famous incidents of frontier life that is reported in most books about that era. The Indian is nearly always reported as named "Big Foot." Eckert insists that is incorrect. In conflicts of this kind I choose to accept Eckert.

Chapter 5
Life in the Midst of Chaos
1773 - 1794

"It was a time of terror unparalleled on a frontier where terror had always been known."
1

And, it went on for twenty-one years, relentlessly, inexorably. The Indian raids were like angry waves smashing again and again against the frontierspeople here in the Ohio country, wiping out families, destroying homes, ravaging this land.

We can't imagine life in those days. Today we travel the highways from Waynesburg to Washington to Pittsburgh, serene and secure as we admire the countryside and go about our jobs and daily activities. Back then we would have passed by burning cabins, mutilated bodies, and enraged, armed men with their women and children, starring at us through bitter, sorrowful eyes. There was no peace, nor safety, nor any tranquillity in Burgettstown, Canonsburg, McKeesport, nor Sewickley, or Mt. Lebanon. Everywhere the people lived with fear - ready to fight or flee in a heartbeat.

And this went on for twenty-one years.

"Everywhere throughout the frontier...settlements were hit and destroyed...and in the area of Fort Pitt and the rivers above it - the Monongahela Valley southward and the Allegheny Northward - destruction was rampant...

Isolated homes, barns and mills were being burned and individuals were being shot from ambush or their families attacked in their homes." 2

It was endless. No matter the year the grim reports tell the same story over and over like a broken record.

In June of 1774 Governor Richard Penn tells of reports he received "by different Expresses from Westmoreland (then, all of western Pennsylvania), all informing him of Sundry Murders, committed on the Frontiers of this Province by the Indians." 3

Col. Archibald Lochry wrote on Nov. 2, 1777: "...the frontier is much distressed, the savages daily committing hostilities, burning and plundering." 4

In the spring of 1780 and just outside of Oakdale, a suburb of Pittsburgh, Dolly Clark and her baby were captured by an Indian war-party. When the baby began to cry the Indians killed it. "The mother, frozen with grief, covered the face of the dead child with her apron and walked on without a tear." 5 She was later rescued by Rangers who followed the trail of the war-party.

Col. Lochry wrote again on July 4, 1781: "We have very distressing times here this summer. The enemy are almost constantly in our country killing and captivating the inhabitants." 6

(He would be killed later that year in fighting with Indians.)

Things were no better in 1782.

The Walker family had a cabin on Robinson's Run (today, on Noblestown Road) near the present borough of Carnegie, a suburb of Pittsburgh. In September of that year (1782) twenty-five Indians attacked the house and some of the older children working in a nearby field. Mrs. Walker saw them coming, grabbed her baby and another small child and ran into some high weeds behind the house. She hid there for a while then quietly slipped away and raced, as best she could with an infant and a toddler, to Ewings Fort, four miles away. Mr. Walker was some distance from the house and was chased by a few of the Indians but he, too, made it to Ewings Fort. In the meantime the five older children, working in the fields, were captured. The Indians then burned the cabin and marched to Ewings Fort with the evident intention of attacking it. Providentially, just when the Indians arrived several armed men from the neighborhood ran into the fort providing much needed reinforcements. The Indians realized that this little fort was now much too strong to attack. So, very callously, and in full view of the people in the fort - including Mr. & Mrs. Walker - they murdered two Walker boys, one eight year old and a twelve year old. Then they left. The men in the fort followed them and caught them trying to cross the Ohio River at Beaver, killed one, wounded another, and dispersed the rest. Two daughters of the Walkers and a son were taken prisoner. These three children were either ransomed or escaped about a year or two later and returned to their family." 7

In 1790 there was more of the same. About 40 miles from Pittsburgh:

"The McIntosh family...were out at some distance from their house engaged in stacking hay or grain, when the Indians fired on them, killing the father on the stack. The mother and six children fled toward the house, but were overtaken, tomahawked and scalped. The daughter...had been sent to a distant pasture with a horse, and hearing the firing, and realizing the danger, fled to Roney's Blockhouse and gave the alarm. Hercules Roney and a party of men started at once for the scene of the butchery. The Indians had gone but the eight dead and mutilated bodies told the bloody tale. Roney and his party buried them on the farm...." 8

This family had lived on Blockhouse Run near Good Intent, just a few miles south of I-70.

One can go forward or backward in time and find these stories repeated hundreds of times:

> "From Pittsburgh south, including the Valleys of the Monongahela and Youghigheny, and the territory west of these to the Ohio...there were few families who had lived therein any considerable length of time that had not lost some of their number by the merciless Indians." 9

It is depressing to read of these things, much less having to live through those days and it is difficult to realize that these settlers had to absorb and survive this horror for such a length of time. '74 was the same as '79 which was identical to '85 which was the twin of '94. Some years were a little worse that others - 1777 earned the sad title of "The Year of the Bloody Sevens" and 1780 was "The Year of Sorrows." They were all bad.

During the Revolution, in 1778, a British Officer described the work of his Huron, Ottawa, and Iroquois allies (some 2300 struck out from Ft. Niagara in war parties large and small):

> "The Indians of the Six Nations and those from the westward have exerted themselves in laying waste the Country most exposed to them, from the east branch of the Susquehanna to the Kiskismenitas Creek upon the Ohio, and thence down (the Ohio) to Kanhawa River, an extent of many hundred miles is now nothing but an heap of ashes; such of those miserable people as have escaped have taken refuge in small forts." 10

That is all of south-western Pennsylvania he is speaking of.

One commentator remarked "Under these circumstances it seems remarkable that any settlements were maintained west of the Allegheny Mountains during the years of the Revolution." 11

There is a certain letter uncovered by the great frontier historian Allan Eckert and set forth in his recent book, That Dark and Bloody River (p. 310) which demonstrates the horror of those days. It is from the British Secretary of Indian Affairs in Albany, New York to the British Governor in Montreal, and is a letter of transmittal accompanying eight bundles of scalps taken by Seneca Indians. Those Indians lived in northwestern Pennsylvania and western New York, and those scalps would have been taken during raids in this area and northern West Virginia. There were a total of 1006 scalps for which the British government would have paid $10,060.00.

The letter reads as follows:

January 3d, 1782

May it please your Excellency,

At the request of the Seneca Chiefs, I herewith send to your Excellency, under the care of James Boyd, eight packages of scalps, cured, dried, hooped and painted with the Indian triumphal marks, of which the following is invoice and explanation:

No. 1. Containing 43 scalps of Congress soldiers, killed in different skirmishes; these are stretched on black hoops 4 inches in diameter; the inside of the skin painted red, with a small black spot to note their being killed by bullets. Also, 62 of farmers killed in their homes; the hoops painted red, the skin painted brown, and marked with a hoe, a dark circle all around to indicate their being surprised at night, and a black hatchet in the middle, signifying their being killed with that weapon.

No. 2. Containing 98 of farmers killed in their houses; hoops red, figure of a hoe to mark their profession, great white circle and sun to show they were surprised in the daytime; a little red foot to show they stood upon their defense, and died fighting for their lives and families.

No. 3. Containing 97 of farmers; hoops green, to show they were killed in the fields; a large white circle with a little round mark on it for the sun, to show it was in the daytime, black bullet mark on some, and hatchet on others.

No. 4. Containing 102 of farmers, mixed of several of the marks above, only 18 marked with a little yellow flame, to denote their being prisoners burned alive after being scalped, their nails pulled out by the roots, and other torments; one of those latter was supposed to be an American clergyman, his hand being fixed to the hoop of the scalp. Most of the farmers appear, by the hair, to be young or middle-aged men, there being but 67 very grey heads among them all; which made the service more essential.

No. 5. Containing 88 scalps of women, hair braided in the Indian fashion to show that they were mothers, hoops blue, skin yellow ground with little red tadpoles to represent, by way of triumph, the tears of grief occasioned to their relations; a black scalping knife or hatchet at the bottom, to mark their being killed by these instruments; 17 others, very grey, black hoops, plain brown color, no marks by the short club or casse-tete, to show they were knocked down dead, or had their brains beat out.

No. 6. Containing 193 boy's ...scalps of various ages, small green hoops, whitish ground on the skin, with red tears in the middle, and black marks, knife, hatchet, or club as their death happened.

No. 7. Containing 211 girls...scalps of various ages, small green hoops, white ground, tears, hatchet, club, scalping knife, etc.

No. 8. This package is a mixture of all the varieties above mentioned, to the number of 122, with a birch box containing 29 little infant's scalps of various sizes, small white hoops, white ground, no tears, and only a little black knife in the middle, to show they were ripped out of their mother's bellies."

These scalps would have been taken in 1781, and that was not the worst year on the frontier.

Albany was not the only "collection point." The biggest one was at Detroit and others were at Presque Isle and Fort Niagara.

How could the frontierspeople, the "Backwoodsmen" have possibly taken this beating? They were very tough people, they had been through it before, and they were damned if they were going to give up their land.

Still there were many people who couldn't stand it and they left. At one time it was reported that as many as a thousand people were lined up at the three ferries across the Monongahela River waiting to cross and go back east. 12 Valentine Crawford wrote to George Washington on May 6, 1774:

"This alarm has caused the people to move from over the Monongahela, off Chartiers and Raccoon (Creeks), as fast as you ever saw them in...1756 or 1757 down in Frederick County...There were more than one thousand people crossed the Monongahela in one day at three ferries that are not one mile apart...On Sunday evening, about four miles over Monongahela, the Indians murdered one family, consisting of six, and took two boys prisoners. At another place they killed three, which makes in the whole nine and two prisoners. If we had not had forts built there would not have been ten families left this side of the mountains besides what are at Fort Pitt." 13

The Negley family had had enough - to the great good fortune of Pittsburgh - because they became one of its leading families.

They had a farm several miles from Ligonier. In the Spring of 1788 Indians swept through that area and they were alerted by scouts to leave and head for Fort Ligonier. There was snow on the ground and Mr. Negley quickly hitched their horse to a sleigh and Mary Ann Negley, seven months pregnant, climbed aboard with Elizabeth, aged six, Peter, aged four, and Margaret, aged two. Her husband and twelve year old son acted as guards. Just as they pulled out from their house the Indians arrived. Mr. Negley and young Jacob fired at the

Indians and delayed them while Mrs. Negley raced for her life along a narrow, rough trail through the trees. It was a running battle with Mr. Negley and Jacob firing, then racing back toward the sleigh, then stopping to fire again - constantly worried that the Indians would get ahead of them and cut off the sleigh. At one awful moment the horse shied at the noise of the rifles, bumped the sled against a rock and broke a shaft. Mary Ann had to stop, climb out, and with desperate, fear-driven fingers, take ten minutes to repair the sled. When they were about one-half mile from the fort her husband roared something to the effect of , "Go for it, give it all it's got" and she beat the horse to a racing frenzy and made it to the gates. Her husband and little Jacob kept firing and running and arrived breathless but safe.

(In retrospect, one sees here the frontier education of a twelve year old boy. He didn't learn about reading and writing - he learned about killing and fighting.)

Mrs. Negley gave birth to a son, John, at Fort Ligonier shortly thereafter.

She adamantly refused to return to the farm and her husband agreed. They moved to Pittsburgh and bought some land along the Allegheny River, land which is now the Highland Park Zoo, and in this relative safety they became quite prosperous and leading members of Pittsburgh society. 14

It was a tough life.

It had never before lasted as long as these bloody two decades and perhaps, in times past, the number of raiders was a little less, but all Indians raids were horrible and were very much the same whether the raiders were Mohawks from Albany, Ottawas from Michigan, or Shawnee from Kentucky, and whether the year was 1755 or 1775.

Suppose for a moment that it is 1773 and that you are a forty year old man or woman, with a spouse and children, who has bought some land near Pittsburgh, Greensburg, Washington, or Beaver, and moved here to live and farm. You would have been born in 1733, perhaps near the frontier towns of Lancaster or Harrisburg. This would have been the story of your life:

1755 - age 22 - Lancaster - General Braddock has just been defeated on the banks of the Monongahela River. The victorious French encouraged their Indian allies to attack the English frontier settlements. That was where you lived. The Indians stormed across the Allegheny Mountains and attacked everywhere in Pennsylvania, Maryland, and Virginia. Your neighbor, Adam Hoops, in Lancaster, would write the Governor of Pennsylvania:

"We are in as bad circumstances as ever any poor Christians were ever in; for the cries of widowers, widows, fatherless and motherless children, are enough to pierce the most hardest of hearts...These deplorable circumstances cry aloud for your

Honor's most wise consideration; for it is really very shocking for the husband to see the wife of his bosom, her head cut off, and the children's blood drunk like water by these bloody and cruel savages." 15

Your Uncle, John Harris, at Harrisburg would be writing Gov. Morris at the same time:

"In the name of God, help us! The inhabitants are abandoning their plantations; and we are in a dreadful situation. The Indians are cutting us off every day...their scouts scalping our families on our frontiers daily." 16

Somehow you survived this madness, and the French and Indian War finally ended, after seven years of hell.

Now the year is 1763 and you are 30 years old, married, with children. You and your family leave Lancaster and head for new lands around Bedford - recently bought from the Indians.

Unbeknownst to you, far off at Detroit, Michigan, an Ottawa chief named Pontiac has stirred up all of the tribes with the idea that if they strike together and all at once they can drive the white man into the Atlantic Ocean. In May of 1763 the blow falls and a horde of Indian raiders come again. Ft. Detroit is besieged, but holds, Ft. Pitt is besieged but it also holds; eleven other widely scattered military forts are destroyed and the Indians are in your front yard and you are, again, fighting for your life. Your Governor, Hamilton, advises the General Assembly on July 4, 1763:

"It is now about a Month since we were alarmed by Accounts ...from Ft. Pitt...Then came the news of the cruel Murders that have since been committed, not only upon our Traders, but upon several new settled Families, far within the purchased parts of the Province, without the least provocation. From a dread of being cruelly Butchered, the miserable People, throughout almost the whole Frontiers of the Province, have been induced to desert their Settlements with the utmost Precipitation, together with all their Worldly Substance, and to take Refuge in the interior Parts, where it cannot be but extremely burdensome to the inhabitants to support them." 17

And this would go on for another year and a half.

So now it is 1773 and you are 40 years old and living on newly purchased land (from the Iroquois) in the Ohio country in the general vicinity of Pittsburgh. You're getting acquainted with the Monongahela River as well as the Youghigheny, Allegheny, and the Ohio. You learn of Chartiers Creek, Buffalo Creek, Ten Mile Creek, and Beaver Creek. There are a few neighbors farming around you.

You think you've seen it all. You have dodged the bullets, fended off the scalping knife, turned aside the tomahawk during two long struggles, and now at age 40 you hope to live in peace. Instead you are about to endure a Deluge of Bloody Terror that will last until you are an old person of sixty-one. You are in for the worst battles of your life - a "time of terror unparalleled on a frontier where terror had always been known."

Eternal vigilance would be required and there would be frightening nights for you and your family. Perhaps a son of yours would live to write of those days:

"I well remember that, when a little boy, the family were sometimes waked up in the dead of night by an express with a report that the Indians were at hand. The express came softly to the door, or back window, and by gently tapping woke the family. This was easily done, as an habitual fear made us ever watchful and sensible to the slightest alarm. The whole family was instantly in motion. My father seized his gun and other implements of war. My stepmother waked up and dressed the children as well as she could, and being myself the oldest of the children I had to take my share of the burdens to be carried to the fort. There was no possibility of getting a horse in the night to aid us in removing to the fort.

Besides the little children, we caught up what articles of clothing and provision we could get hold of in the dark, for we durst not light a candle or even stir the fire. All this was done with the utmost dispatch and the silence of death. The greatest care was taken not to waken the youngest child. To the rest it was enough to say 'Indian,' and not a whimper was heard afterwards." 18

How sad it is that even the little children knew that the word "Indian" was a synonym for terror and death. They, too, had been through it before.

What was it like to live through an Indian raid in this area, in those days? Not many people survived one who could write, or who told their stories to others who did write them down. Of course Mary Jemison, previously quoted, was one but she was only thirteen when she was captured. A more mature report is that of Phoebe Cunningham who was a pert twenty-four year old in 1783 and lived near Fairmont, West Virginia when a war-party of four Wyandots attacked her cabin. She told the story to her granddaughter:

Her husband, Thomas, had gone to Pittsburgh to buy some things but he was expected home that day, August 31, and she had set a place for him at the table. Her four children were with her, Henry, aged four, Lydia, three, Walter, two, and baby Thomas, six months old. Earlier she had washed a beautiful red and white coverlet and placed it on the fence outside to dry. Two Indians came out of the woods and hid by the fence behind the coverlet. Then one of them, "a tall, very fat one, painted for war all red and yellow and black" crossed the yard and entered the house about noon-time. The table was set "with bear-meat, new potatoes, cooked whole, fresh-picked peas, apple-sauce, a fresh-baked vinegar pie and sweet milk." (How strange it is that Phoebe could remember, years later, exactly the food that was on the table.) The Indian ate some potatoes and pie and drank the milk. Then he went to the window and looked toward a nearby house. Just then the neighbor saw the Indian and both men seized their rifles and fired, both missing. The Indian asked Phoebe how many men were in that house and she lied, telling him "ten." He ate some more food, then pulled the ticks off the beds, heaped them together and set the straw on fire. He found some other ticks with feathers in them and he dumped them on the fire creating a thick, black smoke.

Just then the second Indian dashed from behind the coverlet toward the door but Phoebe's neighbor was watching and shot that man, badly wounding him. He crawled back under the fence and disappeared.

The Indian in the house watched his companion get away then turned, pulled out his tomahawk, seized four-year old Henry, smashed his skull with the tomahawk then proceeded to scalp him. "Grandma said as this happened there was not a sound in the house, except those made by the Indian's hatchet and knife and the crackle of the fire."

Then the man grabbed Phoebe, who was holding Thomas, and shoved her out the door, Walter and Lydia clinging to her skirts. As she was pushed toward the woods her neighbor called out that he would go get some help and come after her. Hiding among the trees were two other Indians with the wounded man. They quickly made a litter to carry him. Before starting off they tomahawked and scalped little Walter and taking three-year old Lydia by the legs repeatedly pounded her against a tree until she was dead. Then they scalped her and started off. They traveled some distance and found a cave, the entrance to which they concealed with branches and leaves. They stayed there four days, tending the wounded man until he died. Twice in that time Phoebe heard rescuers passing by, looking for her, but she dared not utter a sound. Then the party headed for the Ohio river. On the ninth day the Indians took the baby, Thomas, chopped it to pieces and left it for the wolves.

Phoebe was taken to a Wyandot town in Ohio where she stayed for three years and was finally ransomed by an English trader and released to return home to her husband - who had never stopped looking for her. 19

Such was an Indian raid.

It is interesting to note the complete lack of emotional expression in the recitation of this horrible experience. This is fairly typical of all such reports. The narrator doesn't even hint of fear, anger, shock or outrage. No mother flies to the defense of her children, the children do not cry or scream; the men do not curse or rage. The story is told in a flat, toneless, bare-bones type of way. Such and such a thing happened, period. Supply the emotions yourself.

There are a few exceptions. Mary Jemison remembers that after her family was captured her father broke down and, during the march with the Indians, repeatedly and openly damned himself for letting it happen. When Mary Francis was butchered by the Indians a survivor tells us about her screams and moans and that the two men who were also cut up and thrown into the pot cursed and damned the Indians in great roars of outrage before they were killed. But, generally, there is a notable silence with regard to any discussion of emotions or feeling.

It's a curiosity.

Phoebe did give us one hint of the depth of her feelings - she did remember, after all those years, that when the Indian killed her son, Walter, "there was not a sound in the house except those made by the Indian's hatchet and knife and the crackle of the fire."

Note, also, the small size of the war-party, only four men. This was often the case. The Indians would come in large parties - thirty to fifty men - then split up into numerous small groups. It was easy to attack a farm family - the man would be out in a nearby field, working, and a prime target for a bullet or arrow fired from the woods. With him dead the war-party could quietly walk up to the house and do as they pleased with the wife and children. It didn't take twenty men to wipe out a farm family, four would do just fine.

Or seven. That's the number who showed up at the Ross cabin one evening on March 21, 1791. The Ross family lived on Bull Creek near Tarentum (a suburb of Pittsburgh) and about three miles from the Allegheny River. The Indians were very polite and left their rifles outside the door, a gesture of friendship. They asked for food, were invited into the house, and were courteously served a dinner at the table. Obviously the white people were apprehensive because gathered at the Ross house - apparently a large, two-story one - were the Dary's along with the Clark and Cutright families. Four families in all. After finishing dinner one of the Indians walked outside, picked up his rifle, then came back into the house, shut the door and stood there, guarding it. The other six warriors grabbed their tomahawks and began slashing and killing. Bedlam broke loose as men and women fought, children screamed and ran about in terror, and the house was filled with fighting, thrashing, dying people. The four white men died first then the Indians turned on the women and children. Mrs. Dary watched in unbelievable horror as an Indian took her eighteen month old child and, using it as a club, repeatedly bashed its head against the skull of Grandma Ross until both were dead, the old woman being finished off with a tomahawk blow. With fear and rage giving her strength, Mrs. Dary hurled aside the Indian at the door and tore it open. The Indian slashed her in the side of her face with his tomahawk leaving a terrible, bleeding gash and momentarily stunning her, but she got out the door and three of her daughters raced after her. Jacob Dary, aged six, ran too, found a nearby log, crawled under it and lay still. In the wild turmoil Agnes Clark fought her way out the door with two children and so did Catherine Cutright, but she left behind a dead husband and son. John Dary, aged fourteen, ran outside and hid in a hollow tree. The Indians were too busy to stop them. It takes time and considerable effort to kill four men, two women (Mrs. Ross and Grandma Ross) and six children; then more time to scalp them and plunder the cabin. In the dark night the surviving women and children ran and ran in what must have been a mad, frenzied flight the three long miles to the Allegheny River at Tarentum. There they gathered on shore and screamed for help to Levi Johnston whose cabin stood across the river. He heard them, shoved his canoe into the water, and made repeated trips across the river to ferry these survivors to the eastern shore. Since the canoe could only take a few people at a time, what must have been the terrible fear wracked feelings of those left behind while Levi, paddling with all his strength, crossed back and forth over that broad stretch of water?

Levi's cabin was no safe haven. There was a fort nine miles away and they all started for it at once, now accompanied by Levi and his family. It was very cold - there was a frost that night - and through the woods trudged a shocked, desperate caravan. They ran and walked twelve miles that night, measuring from the Ross cabin. They made it.

That was an Indian raid.

And once again the searing flames of implacable hatred for Indians was burned into the hearts and minds of those survivors, of Levi Johnston and his family, of all the people who received them at the fort, and neighbors for miles around.

Tears amid broken hearts were a constant part of frontier life.

Mary Rose Kaneade was a beautiful, blue-eyed, blond of eighteen who was engaged to Danny Yeager. Danny had given her a "whittled wooden ring" as a sign of his love. He decided to leave this area (they lived in what is now northern West Virginia) and go to Kentucky to look for better land. He never came back. A survivor told Mary Rose about his death. She wrote a beautiful, sorrowful, ode to her lover, and directed it to us:

"Secret hearts, I had a lover, Oh, yes! A long time ago.

He went down to Kantucky a long time ago.

He was with Jim Boon, Dave Boon's boy, and Henry Russell a long time ago in Kantucky.

Was it night, so very dark, and in the woods, the wild wolves watching, a long time ago?

Where was Jesus? Oh save poor Danny's soul.

Poor Jim Boon, so young; poor Henry Russell, so young; poor Danny Yeager, so young. Their dreams were broken by the bullets of the Red Men. The poor bodies they chopped and burnt and cut. They screamed and prayed - but Jesus. Where was Jesus? All day to noon they screamed and prayed, so tortured by the Red Men.

They died a long time ago;

Oh! A long time ago.

At the parting Danny gave me a white ribbon and a whittled wooden ring and held my hand and promised to come back and carry me to Kantucky in the springtime, a long time ago.

Oh, can I stand It? Oh, can I stand it?

In the whispers at the window and in the grass and in the shade of the trees and by the waters, I hear Danny. Oh, poor Danny.

I hear Danny in the whispers, all the hours in the night time by the windows. In the whispers, there is my Danny.

Oh, where was Jesus, in Kantucky, a long time ago." [20]

Mary Rose never married.

Some women fought back successfully. Ann (or Anna, sometimes) Hupp was one of them. She was 25 years old on March 30, 1782, and was a true daughter of the frontier. Her maiden name had been Rowe and she had lost her mother and two brothers to an Indian raid by Shawnees six years before. A younger brother, Jacob, had escaped the attack and had come to live with her. He was now sixteen. Ann was married, had three children and was eight-months pregnant with the fourth.

She and her family were in Miller's Blockhouse (about forty miles from Pittsburgh) this day, together with Jacob Miller, Sr., and his family and the Edward Gaither family and a "useless old man" named Mathias Ault.

This was a typical frontier arrangement for defense against Indians. The three families would have worked together to build this blockhouse on Jacob Miller's property, making a two-story cabin, surrounding it and the nearby spring with a stockade fence and putting in such provisions as they felt necessary. Then the Hupps and Gaithers went off to their own houses and farms. When word came of "Indians" everyone would rush to the blockhouse and stay there for as long as necessary - sometimes for months. For the Gaithers and Hupps the Miller Blockhouse would be their safe refuge.

In the early morning of Easter Sunday (March 31) of 1782, several of the men left to go scouting for Indians and headed for Rice's Fort - a similar "settler's-fort" about two miles away.

Later John Hupp, Ann's husband, and Jacob Miller decided to go search for a lost colt. They had gone only about 300 yards when they were ambushed by a Shawnee war-party. It was a large one, about thirty warriors. They quickly killed Hupp and Miller and headed for the Blockhouse.

The three women and the old man heard the firing and guessed at once what had happened.

The Indians spread out when they arrived and began firing. Ann fired back. Loading and re-loading as fast as her nervous fingers would allow, Ann moved from loop-hole to loop-hole aiming and firing, trying to give the impression that several defenders were in the blockhouse and that it was too strong to attack. For three dreadful hours she kept up this charade. Undoubtedly the other women helped - keeping the many children quiet and as calm as possible, peering out the port-holes to locate a careless warrior and calling Ann's attention to his position and, perhaps, re-loading the rifle if Ann was distracted for a moment by the cries or needs of her own children. They all knew that a horrible death awaited them and the children if the Indians got inside.

It was a long, frantic afternoon.

The Indians kept up their firing, but Ann's ruse was working and they held back from a direct assault.

The desperate women had to get word to their men at Rice's Fort and they selected ten year old Fred Miller to make the attempt.

In retrospect this is testimony to the terrible danger they were in and one wonders at the feelings of Mrs. Miller who agreed to let her son make the attempt.

A ten year old is still a child and he was being asked to sneak past the Indians scattered throughout those woods and then to keep going for two more miles. If he was seen the Indians would kill him in a second.

It was a hopeless task and turned out to be so. Young Fred had progressed about two or three hundred yards when he was discovered. He turned and started racing back with two Indians chasing him. The women must have watched with horror. It is strange the things one remembers at a time like that. Every commentator talks about the fence that stood between the running child and the Blockhouse and how, when he got to it, Fred put one hand on the top rail and cleared it in an instant and kept going for the stockade gate. Then a bullet hit his left arm just at a moment when it was flexed so that the bullet went through his bicep then shattered the bone between the elbow and wrist. Panting and bleeding he charged through the open gate and into his mother's arms.

The Indians behind him veered off when they came close to the stockade.

At Rice's Fort down the valley, the sound of the firing was finally heard and Jacob Miller, Jr., Philip Hupp, and young sixteen year old Jacob Rowe started back to the scene of the firing. When they approached the women saw them and signaled with white handkerchiefs the best way for them to approach so as to avoid most of the Indians. In the event they ran right past a few Indians who were so surprised they didn't even fire as the men ran safely into the fort.

With this additional firepower the besieged families were able to force a stalemate until dark. Then the Indians got bored and went away sometime during the night. [21]

The next day they found the bodies of Jacob Miller, Sr. and John Hupp and buried them in the graveyard behind the blockhouse. That graveyard is still there today and a picture of it is with the description of Miller's Blockhouse.

In this maelstrom of violence women often had to fight and fend for themselves. Their men were frequently gone from the house to work in a distant field, or on a hunting trip, or off to a distant town for supplies. The woman was alone, with her children, and if she saw the Indians coming and had a weapon she used it. It was a matter of fight or die. The problem, of course, was that the Indian was a master of stealth and rarely gave the women a chance to resist. As Phoebe Cunningham could testify the warrior was in the house before she knew he was around.

The struggle of Experience Bozarth is illustrative. Her home was the neighborhood fort on Dunkard Creek in (now) Greene County. She and the other families had "forted-up" due to the presence of raiding parties. On the day in question, April 1, 1789, nearly everyone was gone, for some good reason, except Experience, two men, and several children. Perhaps Experience was "baby-sitting" that day and the two men stayed to help guard the place. Suddenly a band of Shawnee or Wyandots came charging out of the forest. The first notice was the cries of the children playing in the yard. One of the men in the house ran to the door where he was immediately shot in the side and fell to the floor. The warrior who shot him then stepped over his body, came into the house and engaged in a wrestling duel with the other white man. That man hurled the Indian onto the bed and screamed for Experience to bring him a knife. She grabbed a small hand-axe and proceeded to crush the skull of the Indian on the bed. At that moment a second Indian came into the room and shot dead the white man struggling at the bedside. Experience then charged this man with her axe slicing open his abdomen so that his intestines spilled onto the floor. He screamed in pain and for help. The other members of the war-party had been chasing and killing the children in the yard and now they came rushing to the assistance of their comrade. As one of them came into the doorway Experience split his skull with her axe and he fell outside. The wounded Indian crawled to the door where his comrades seized him and dragged him outside. At this time the white man who had been shot in the side revived, struggled to his feet, and he and Experience managed to shut the door and pull down the bar to lock it. Experience and her wounded companion stayed in the house for two days until a relief party arrived. The presence of two dead bodies in the cabin and some dead children in the yard outside must have added immeasurably to the ugliness of this experience. 22

The instances of women fighting at their homes or in the nearby fields are as numerous as the Indian raids that made them necessary.

Let me tell you one more such story, a famous tale that lingered for many years but is now long-forgotten like the others. It involved a teen-ager named Elizabeth Zane whose home was close to Wheeling, West Virginia, near Fort Henry. On September 1, 1777, nearly three hundred Indians appeared out of the morning mist and attacked the fort and the homes near it. In the Ebenezer Zane house were four men, three women, and seven little children. They fought back. In mid-afternoon the supply of powder in the Zane house began to run very low and those people were in desperate circumstances. They knew there was powder in the fort but that was sixty long dangerous yards away. It was doubtful whether anyone could get through the Indian rifle fire to get to the fort, much less get back.

Betty volunteered to go. The house door was opened a little and out she ran as fast as she ever ran in her life. The Indians were so startled at this sudden, racing apparition that only a few of them grasped what was happening and fired. Betty made it into the fort. There they gave her a cask of powder which she could barely lift to her shoulder much less run with. However, she wore an apron and had an idea. She made a pouch of the apron and into it was poured about two-thirds of the cask of powder. Betty tied the apron ends together and grasping this heavy and awkward package stepped out of the gate and began her desperate race. The Indians were ready. Sixty yards is a long way to go when people are shooting at you. There were no trees to hide or shield her, it was an open course. Betty ran while bullets splattered the ground around her, some going through her flying skirt as she zigzagged her way toward the house. Breathless and arms weary from the weight of the powder she dashed into the open door. That powder was worth more to her family than all of the gold in the world.

The fight lasted all day and part of the next, then the Indians disappeared into the forest. It was over.

During the wars of this Twentieth Century there have been many stories of brave men risking their lives dashing through enemy fire to get ammunition for their comrades. Often they were rewarded with a distinguished medal - The Silver Star - for this heroic act.

Betty Zane did it. Her reward was life itself and the love of her family. She received no medal.

(Incidentally, of the Indians who disappeared about one-hundred of them headed north into Pennsylvania and attacked Rice's Fort in Washington County. They caused settlers to "fort-up" at Lamb's Fort, and threw a scare into those at Doddridge's Fort when they burnt and plundered nearby cabins and killed anyone who was not in a fort. These stories are told in the section dealing with those particular forts.)

We, the current generation of Americans, are duty bound, out of respect for these frontiers-people, to reflect for a few moments about these experiences. These were not mere adventures, they were terrible life and death struggles. Ann Hupp fought back in 1782; Phoebe Cunningham saw her four children murdered in 1783; Mary Ann Negley raced for her life in 1788, and Experience Bozarth engaged in mortal combat in 1789. These years weren't even the worst ones - recall that 1777 was the Year of the Bloody Sevens and 1780 was the Year of Sorrows.

The hatred of Indians that these struggles ignited and kept a roaring blaze cannot even be imagined. Ann Hupp and Mary Ann Negley each had a baby one month after these experiences and Phoebe Cunnignham had three more children. Can it be doubted that as these mothers nursed their babies they fed them not only nourishment but also a fierce hatred of Indians?

The effect on the children must have been equally corrosive. Ann Hupp's brother, Jacob Rowe, was ten years old when he saw his mother and oldest brother killed by Shawnee and a younger brother captured. Jacob made his escape and suffered terribly while he traveled, terribly alone and very frightened, for seventy miles to the home of his sister. At age sixteen, gun in hand, he raced to Miller's Blockhouse to defend her against another group of Shawnee. Can it be doubted that he hated those Indians and had good cause for such feelings?

Fred Miller was only ten years old when, under fire, he was sent to try to sneak through the lines of those same Shawnee to get help and he received a crippled arm and searing memories for his efforts.

Jacob Negley was twelve years old when he fought and ran, side by side with his father, to protect his mother and three brothers and sister.

Recall the words of Rev. Doddridge that as one woke up the children in the dead of night that "it was enough to say 'Indian" and not a whimper was heard afterwards."

The hatred of Indians was congenital on the frontier and was totally justified by the hideous sufferings those people had to endure at the hands of Indian warriors.

Never in the last two hundred years, has a woman in this area had to suffer hearing the screams of her children being murdered in her front yard while she fights for her life in the living room. Frontier women lived this - not once in a lifetime - but repeatedly for thirty years. Their hatred of Indians was very much a part of their being.

Life was hard, bloody, and cruel but no one could cry forever. The fields had to be plowed, planted, and cared for; the women had cows to milk, a vegetable garden to tend, weaving, sewing, and child-rearing to keep them busy. The numbers of children indicate that time was found for loving.

Keziah Batten Shearer remembers it this way:

"The living in the old times was hard. Women and children cried a great deal and the men and boys cussed a lot. And everybody prayed enough, in church, in the fields, wherever and whenever they had the feeling for it. But mostly we all just laughed, about nothing much to eat, I mean, and the Indians sneaking around...."

And we abided, and it was wonderful....Hard working men and women are hard-loving, too. And that's what it takes to make the mare go - hard-working and hard-loving. We was lonesome a lot. Everybody was lonesome, I guess in the old times. The woods caused it. The woods were gloomy, but of a morning and evening they were kind of grand too. We put up with a lot of trouble, but we stayed brave, and God was by us every minute, you know..." 23

These people had faith in their God and in themselves and with these they hung on and survived.

We can only shake our heads in wonder and ask - how did they do it?

There were fun times - weddings, games, house-warmings, church meetings when neighbors would get together for prayer and sociability, business trips to Pittsburgh, uproarious political rallies with plenty of hard-liquor at hand, and dances. One very romantic, gay, and touching story is related in a letter from a young British officer stationed at Fort Pitt in 1763 to his commander, Col. Bouquet, who was apparently elsewhere at the time:

"We are all in high spirits here, And as we have News so seldom from the Busy world, we Amuse ourselves weekly not only with a Club But a Grand Assembly. The Last Night we Mustered 12 or 13 Couples Old, and Young, for you must know the Mothers and Grandmothers, Attend to vouch for the Chastity of their Daughters, as well as be their Guardians for the Night as we have none but those of the Strictest Virtue. But Croghan (George Croghan, the old trader) Generally pushed About the Glass so Copiously and briskly amongst the Old Women that before half the Night's over they forget their Errand as well as their Charge, and what then follows is easily guest at." 24

Ah, Romance! Young people never change.

There was even good cheer in the face of an expected Indian attack. At Doddridge's the families had "forted-up" because Indians were close at hand burning cabins and pillaging. An attack on the fort was expected the next morning and Capt. Teter was elected to be their commander. He gave orders to the men and women regarding preparations for this anticipated attack. The women were to haul water from the spring in every available vessel and place it at many strategic spots. This was to enable the defenders to put out fires if the Indians shot fire-arrows at the fort building, the nearby cabins, or the stockade fence. The women also had to cut cloth patches for the men to use when firing their rifles, and melt lead to mold bullets for the rifles. As Rev. Doddridge describes it:

"The ladies of the present day will suppose that our women were frightened half to death, with the near prospect of such an attack of the Indians; on the contrary, I do not know that I ever saw a merrier set of women in my life. They went on with their work of carrying water and cutting bullet patches for the men without the least emotion of fear, and I have every reason to believe that they would have been pleased with the crack of the guns in the morning." 25

People can be cheerful even in the most trying of circumstances and these settler families could find happiness in many aspects of their daily lives.

This episode does point out the defensive nature of the frontiers-peoples' reaction to Indian attacks. As was mentioned in the last chapter, an offensive response was rare. In the thirty year period between 1765 and 1795 you could count on your fingers and toes - and have digits left over - the number of expeditions, military or civilian, against Indian villages. Never was there a wholesale slaughter of Indian women and children such as the Indians did to the white frontiers-people. There is not one single instance of a successful attack on a hostile Indian village and the killing of its women and children. Not one. That is amazing.

It is a tribute to the skills of the Indian warriors - and their adept use of diplomacy.

The current concept of the Indians as helpless, hapless, defenseless victims of cruel white people is simply obscene. What an insult! The Indian warriors were robust, skilled, and brutal and, today, to pretend that they were spineless "victims" is an unconscionable assault on their ability and pride.

Oh, the white people tried to attack them from time to time and their hatred might have resulted in wholesale slaughter, but it never happened. That kind of killing was a one-way street - from the Indians to the settlers.

The Indians used three successful strategies to repel white invaders:

1. They ambushed and defeated an attacking force;

2. They took their women and children and withdrew into the forest, allowing   the soldiers to destroy an empty village;

3. They sued for peace and got it - then did whatever was necessary to get the army to withdraw.

All three were effective. At no time were their women and children killed in these attacks.

Some mention ought to be made of "scalp bounties," another effort to get back at the Indians. Way back in 1756 Pennsylvania offered a bounty on Indian scalps. It did no good and was abandoned a year later. Why? The Indians were far superior to white men in the business of collecting scalps. As Francis Parkman put it: "Rewards were offered for prisoners and scalps (of Indians), so bountiful that the hunting of men would have been a profitable vocation, but for the extreme wariness and agility of the game." 26 Very few settlers - and none of the many foreign immigrants - had the forestry and war-like skills to go off into the woods fifty to two hundred miles, skulk around an Indian village killing people for their scalps, and then return to collect some money. It couldn't be done. Even if one wandered around the forests here in western Pennsylvania trying to kill Indians who might be out hunting, the odds were great that the Indians would find you before you found them and that it would be your scalp that would be lifted. That the Indians were good at this is illustrated by the fact that, for just three raids, the British paid $2940.00 in gold and silver for 294 white scalps, and an observer once saw a large dry-goods box half-filled with scalps of white people. 27 That was a lot of scalps.

In desperation, Pennsylvania tried the experiment again in 1780 and kept the statute in effect until March 21, 1783. The records of payments in this area show one payment of twelve pounds ten shillings to Adam Poe for one scalp on April 2, 1781, and a payment of twenty-five pounds to Alexander Wright and William Minor for two scalps on March 21, 1783, and a payment to Sam Brady on Feb. 19, 1781, of twelve pounds, ten shillings for one scalp. 28 The failure of the policy can be summed up in these words:

"Furthermore the offer (of scalp bounties) was practically a dead letter, for President Reed (of the Pennsylvania Supreme Executive Council) repeatedly said that it was barren of results. Nor must the fact be overlooked that Congress had not sanctioned it, and that Continental officers refused to let it go into effect where they had jurisdiction." 29

There are no records to be found anywhere of substantial payments to "bounty hunters" nor of dozens of Indian scalps being turned in for payment. It just didn't happen.

Punitive expeditions were mounted from time to time that did no good for the reasons previously given. Lord Dunmore, from Williamsburg, declared a "war" on the Shawnee in 1774 and this is one of the rare instances in which there was a climactic battle. It occurred at Point Pleasant in (todays) West Virginia and the Shawnee were badly mauled. They sued for a peace that lasted for about five minutes (historically speaking). As soon as the white man army left the Shawnee went back to raiding the settlers, and indeed during the Revolution which began two years later, and until 1794, they were prominent in the raids in this area.

Pennsylvania launched a raid against the Seneca in 1779, up the Allegheny River from Pittsburgh to Franklin and it was typical - the Indians saw the small, six-hundred man army coming, took their families off into the woods, and the army was left to destroy empty villages, burn some crops, and kill very few Indians. They did have one fight with forty warriors coming down the river and did some damage there.

Col. William Crawford tried a raid into Ohio against the Wyandots and Delawares in 1782 and it was a disaster. The Indians watched him coming, set up an ambush, routed his men and had a good time collecting white-man scalps. They captured Crawford and tortured him to death as has been described elsewhere in this book.

Finally, there was the great Sullivan Expedition of 1779 against the Iroquois. Gen. Sullivan had a well-trained, organized army of 3500 men and he invaded the heartland of that tribe. There was one minor battle at Newtown (now, Elmira) New York, and after that the Indians gathered up their families and disappeared into the woods. As the troops of Sullivan entered village after village they found it deserted - they often didn't even see an Indian - and they had to content themselves with burning the village and the crops in the fields and cutting down the orchards. But they didn't kill Iroquois warriors much less any women and children.

And the Iroquois kept on raiding.

In 1764 Col. Bouquet launched a campaign against the Delaware and Shawnee in Ohio. When he got close to their villages they simply asked for peace negotiations and got them. The army stopped, the villages were untouched.

One way or another - by ambush, flight into the woods, or the skillful use of diplomacy the Indians protected their families. Then, when the white man's army was either destroyed or left they went back to raiding the settlers.

The two stories of atrocities by the frontiersmen that are told and re-told (because there are no others) are the Greathouse Affair and the Moravian Massacre.

In the one a lout named Greathouse, with companions, lured a group of Indian men and women to a party - some say a drinking binge. They then massacred those people and when other Indians, across the river, came to help they also were shot. Twenty-one Indians were killed. 30

In the Moravian Affair, David Williamson led a small group of frontiersmen to the peaceful Delaware Indian village of Gnadenhutten in Ohio. He believed - correctly as it turned out - that war parties were using this place as a "half-way house" - a resting place when going to and returning from their raids on the settlements. They killed about ninety men, women, and children.

Both Greathouse and his gang and the Moravian Murderers were promptly and loudly denounced by the settlers and the men were disgraced in their communities.

These are the only two such incidents that occurred in a thirty year period and they stand in stark contrast to the hundreds of raids by the Indians and the thousands of people they killed, wounded and captured. In addition, whereas the settlers denounced Greathouse and Williamson, the Indians praised their warriors for bringing home the scalps of white children and women. To compare white-man atrocities with Indian atrocities is to compare a drive-by shooting with the Oklahoma City bombing.

It is to the credit of the settlers that they condemned the murder of the ninety men, women, and children whom Williamson and his men killed. We have to wonder, though - how could this be when hatred of Indians was so wide-spread? We forget that when the white people came here they carried a rifle in one hand but they carried a Bible in the other. That Bible was very important to them as were the few ministers in their midst. In fact the first community structure they erected was a church. Sunday -Go To Meeting Day - was a major event. They were so determined to get to church that they went despite Indian raiding parties, and under armed guards, and when even the preacher kept his rifle close by as he began the service. The people took to heart the Christian virtues of love, forgiveness, charity, and understanding. Now, of course, it was impossible not to be filled with hatred and rage when you picked up the bloody remains of your child from the front yard, but that did not extend to Indian women and children. In fact, most settlers rarely saw such people since the villages were so far away. A certain amount of Christian charity could extend to them. White men who killed women and children were thought of as descending to the low-level of the Indian. It was "savage," "barbaric" conduct. Thus the killing of the Delaware Moravians was despicable, and so recognized at the time.

Indian men represented a different story. You could kill them any time and any place and few would speak out against it. Even when hostile Indian chiefs were summoned to Pittsburgh (or elsewhere) for negotiations with governmental authorities they had to be protected. If the settlers ever got to them they killed them, instantly and mercilessly. Indian men were "human devils," "monsters," and if a few good ones were killed amongst the bad ones that's too bad but nobody shed any tears over it.

That Moravian incident deserves a little more discussion. It is very interesting. Those people were a group of about four hundred Christianized, mostly Delaware, Indians under the leadership of two German Moravian missionaries named Zeisberger and Heckewelder. They lived in three villages in eastern Ohio, one of which was Gnadenhutten. They were a classic example of a people who tried to play off "both ends against the middle" and ended up getting burned. The hostile Delawares and Wyandots thought they were spies for the settlers - tipping them off about forthcoming raids. That was true. The settlers thought their villages provided "half-way houses" (rest camps) for war-parties going to and coming from the settlements. That was true. So, both sides were mad at them.

In the fall of 1781 about three hundred angry warriors showed up at Gnadenhutten, burnt the village, destroyed the crops, and forced the people to move to western Ohio. In that winter of 1781-1782 many of them starved to death. Their Indian brothers and sisters didn't care. Then in late '81 or early '82 a number of survivors drifted back to Gnadenhutten. In February 1782, some war-parties raided the settlements. This was unheard of! Indians didn't raid in the winter time. Williamson, and others, deduced that the warriors had come from the west, stopped over at Gnadenhutten, and used it as a base of operations for their raids. Sadly, that turned out to be true. In fact, one of the men on the expedition was Robert Wallace whose wife and three children had just been taken prisoner by Indians. As the frontiersmen marched along they found, on the trail, the body of Mrs. Wallace and her baby, each impaled on a sharpened sapling. This discovery caused fury among the men. When the frontiersmen got to that village they found women's clothing and household implements that they recognized as having been taken from their, or a neighbors, home. Needless to say that discovery inflamed them even more. The Moravian Indians may not have participated in the raids, but they certainly shared in the plunder and the responsibility for the atrocities.

It was a bad scene. An important aspect of it is that it was condemned. [31]

Even as late as 1791 Pittsburgh and all of the area around it was severely raided by the Indians. The Revolutionary War had been over for several years and Fort Pitt had fallen into ruins, but Indians still came from the north, west, and south spreading their terror.

George Washington was now President of the United States, and he heard the cries of the settlers, and he issued orders in late 1791 - Rebuild Fort Pitt! And it was done. Major Craig reported from Pittsburgh on May 18, 1792:

> "Capt. Hughes, with his detachment, has occupied his barracks in the new fort since the 1st instant. Two of the six-pounders are very well mounted in the second story of one of the block-houses. The others will be mounted in a few days. The work, if you have no objection, I will name Fort La Fayette!" [32]

So, once it was Fort Duquesne, then Fort Pitt, and, finally, Fort La Fayette.

Most people don't even know that it ever existed under that name.

The Indian raids didn't change and neither did the frontierspeople. Major Craig sent this urgent report from Pittsburgh a year earlier, on March 25, 1791.

"In consequence of a number of people killed and several taken prisoners by the Indians, in the vicinity of this place, within a few days past, and frequent reports of large parties of savages being on our frontier, the people of this town have made repeated applications for arms and ammunition to me, which I have hither-to refused; but in a town meeting held yesterday, it was resolved that the principal men of the town should wait on me and request a loan of a hundred muskets with bayonets and cartouch boxes ...<u>but in case of my refusal to comply with their requisition, it was resolved to break open the stores and take such a number as they might think proper</u>." 33

The settlers got their guns.

One can hear the distant roar of approval from the Paxton Boys, and James Smith, the Black Rifle, from Lazarus Stewart and Frederick Stump.

The wild days and the willful people were still a part of the frontier.

And this went on until 1794. Then the Federal Government gathered together the money, men and equipment needed and sent General "Mad Anthony" Wayne off for a climactic battle with the Delaware, Wyandot, Huron, Shawnee, Potawatomi, Chippewa, Ottawa, and anyone else who wanted to fight. Wayne had a sizable army, well-trained and equipped, and ready to fight, looking for a fight. Most of them were frontiersmen who had seen too many women and children butchered, were sick of burying men who had been inhumanly tortured to death and were tired of the smell and sight of burning cabins. They marched to an area known as the Fallen Timbers in western Ohio where a fierce storm had once knocked down the trees. There, along the Maumee River, on August 4, 1794, they had it out and the Indians were crushed.

It was all over. The bloody raiding and slaughter in western Pennsylvania had, at last, come to an end.

And you - that mythical settler, born in Lancaster in 1733 and now living near Pittsburgh in 1794, at age sixty-one, you now had your peace, security, and tranquillity. You could sit in your rocker and regale the grandchildren with the tales of "how it used to be." You could, that is, if you survived.

It would have been quite a life - one most of us would prefer to read about rather than live through.

The Rangers and the militia, together with those little settler's forts, enabled the frontierspeople to hang on and survive - though just barely.

The horrors of their daily life must leave us amazed at their tenacity and determination. Out of this red-hot crucible came a brave people with strong ideas and ideals, all of which have inured to our benefit. Without their bloody struggle we wouldn't be here today nor would we have the freedoms we cherish. We owe everything to those people and rarely appreciate the blood, sweat, and tears they expended for us.

It is time to take one moment to say "thank you."

Thank you Ann Hupp - and you, too, Samuel Brady.

NOTES

Five: LIFE IN THE MIDST OF CHAOS

1. Allan W. Eckert, *Wilderness War* (Boston, Mass.: Little, Brown and Company, 1978), p. 285.
2. Ibid.
3. Joseph J. Kelley, Jr., *Pennsylvania: The Colonial Years, 1681-1776* (Garden City, NY: Doubleday & Company, Inc., 1980), p. 695.
4. Reuben Gold Thwaites and Louise Phelps Kellogg, Ed's, *Frontier Defense On The Upper Ohio, 1777-1778* (Madison, Wis.: Wisconsin Historical Society, 1912), p. 147.
5. C. Hale Sipe, *Fort Ligonier and Its Times* (Arno Press & The New York Times, 1971), p. 500; this is a reprint edition of the original published in 1932 by the Telegraph Press, Harrisburg, Pa.
6. Thomas Lynch Montgomery (ed.), *Frontier Forts of Pennsylvania, Vol. II, 2d ed.* (Evensville, Ind.: Unigraphic, Inc., 1978, originally published 1916, Harrisburg, Pa.), p. 380.
7. C. Hale Sipe, *The Indian Wars of Pennsylvania* (Lewisburg, Pa..: Wennawoods Publishing, 1995), pp. 671-672; originally published in 1931, Harrisburg, Pa.
8. Montgomery, ed. *Frontier Forts, Vol. II*, pp. 419-420.
9. Ibid., p. 403.
10. Thwaites and Kellogg, ed's, *Frontier Defense On The Upper Ohio*, pp. 173-174, f.n. 38.
11. Ibid.
12. Boyd Crumrine, *History of Washington County* (Philadelphia, Pa.: L.H. Everts & Co., 1882), p. 69.
13. Ibid.
14. Sipe, *The Indian Wars of Pennsylvania*, p. 845.
15. Allan W. Eckert, *Wilderness Empire* (Boston, Mass.: Little, Brown and Company, 1969), p. 351.
16. Ibid.
17. Kelly, p. 475.
18. Joseph Doddridge, *The Settlement and Indian Wars of the Western Parts of Virginia and Pennsylvania, 1763 - 1783* (Bowie, Maryland: Heritage Books, Inc., 1988; reprinted in 1912, Pittsburgh, Pa; originally published in 1824), p. 95.
19. Glenn D. Lough, *Now And Long Ago* (Morgantown, W.Va.: Morgantown Printing & Binding Co., 1969), pp. 609-613.
20. Ibid., p. 21.
21. Jared C. Lobdell, ed., *Indian Warfare in Western Pennsylvania and Northern West Virginia at the Time of the American Revolution* (Bowie, Md.: Heritage Books, Inc., 1992), pp. 144-152.
    This event was one of the famous ones on the frontier and is mentioned in most books about this era. This is the best account, by Dr. John Hupp who was aged two, and at the blockhouse, when the fight occurred. He probably heard the story 101 times from family, friends, and neighbors as he grew up. See also *Frontier Forts, Vol. II*, p. 413; *Ft. Ligonier and Its Times*, p. 551; *Indian Wars of Pennsylvania*, p. 655, and there are many other references.
22. Sipe, *Indian Wars of Pennsylvania*, p. 586.
23. Lough, pp. 40-41.
24. Alfred Procter James and Charles Morse Stotz, *Drums In The Forest* (Pittsburgh, Pa.: The Historical Society of Western Pennsylvania, 1958), p. 109.
25. Doddridge, p. 223.

26. Francis Parkman, *France and England In North America, Vol. VIII Montcalm and Wolfe, Part I* (New York, N.Y.: Frederick Ungar Publishing Co., 1965), p. 422.

27. Eckert, *Wilderness War*, p. 460, f.n. 220; Allan W. Eckert, *That Dark and Bloody River* (New York, NY: Bantam Books, 1995), p. 696, f.n. 448.

28. Sipe, *Fort Ligonier*, p. 508; Earle R. Forrest, *History of Washington County, Pennsylvania*(Chicago, Ill.: S.J. Clarke Publishing Company, 1926), p. 160.

29. Lewis S. Shimmell, *Border Warfare In Pennsylvania* (Harrisburg, Pa.: R.L. Myers & Company, 1901), p. 70.

30. Eckert, *Dark and Bloody River*, p. 665, f.n. 199.

31. I.D. Rupp, *Early History of Western Pennsylvania* (Lewisburg, PA: Wennawoods Publishing, 1995; originally published, 1846, Harrisburg, Pa.), p. 202 et. seq.; Eckert, *Dark and Bloody River*, pp. 241, 264 et seq.

32. Montgomery, ed., *Frontier Forts, Vol. II*, p. 158-159.

33. Ibid., p. 155.

PART II

<u>THE FORTS</u>

Chapter 6

The Forts - Design and Daily Life

"The people of the border were forced into forts which dotted the country in every direction." 1

"...the country ...is now nothing but an heap of ashes; such as those miserable people as have escaped have taken refuge in small forts."2

Those little forts were the salvation of the frontiers people. They weren't much to look at, many of them were poorly sited from a military point of view and they were quite small - but, they worked. Just let a few men and women get into their fort, arm them with that deadly Pennsylvania Rifle, and they could, and did, hold off Indian raiding parties of all sizes, from five to fifty warriors.

The Indian was no fool. He didn't travel all the way from Detroit, Michigan or Buffalo, New York to die in the cleared, open "killing field" of one or two hundred feet that extended around these forts. Those warriors rarely participated in a grand frontal assault such as Pickett's Charge at Gettysburg. They preferred to fight in the woods, or from the woods, each man with face and body painted so that he was nearly invisible amidst the leaves and underbrush. Ambush and the stealthy approach were their favorite games. If these didn't work they would sometimes risk a public appearance by a few men, under a flag of truce, who would issue loud threats or deceitful promises of safety to try to induce a surrender. Sometimes it worked and a frightful massacre of the fort's inhabitants would then ensue. On another occasion the warriors might stage a phony attack by a small number of their group followed by a quick withdrawal to tempt the angry settlers out of the forts and into the woods where they would be swiftly surrounded and annihilated.

When the Indian failed in these tactics he was at a loss what to do. He had no artillery to batter down the walls of these wooden buildings. Siege warfare was really not in his nature - too long and boring. What next? Usually they would weary of the game and go away. This would be especially true if they had sustained a few casualties. Indians didn't react well to casualties and would withdraw quickly if only two or three men in a war-party were killed or wounded.

All that the settlers had to do was to stay in the fort and keep firing. Their biggest concern was to run out of lead, powder, or water.

The forts were built by and for only a small number of families, usually three or four of them. It was designed to protect only those families, not the whole neighborhood. These farm-families lived not more than two or three miles from "their fort." When the alarm came a woman and her children - many of them infants and toddlers - had to walk there as fast as possible. They could travel two or three miles in one hour which was often the most time they would have before the war-party began to arrive. Completely aside from the time element, little children and a woman carrying a baby can't be expected to walk much further, quickly.

There is no mention in the literature concerning how it was decided that a fort would be erected on the property of a particular person. We can pretty safely assume that the people would discuss the matter, choose that property which was most central among their farms, and agree to build the fort at that site. Having agreed on that matter the next decision would be the type of fort they would erect. In this they would be guided by their experiences with Indian raids "back East."

The Reverend Doddridge tells us that in this area the forts were always one of three different kinds depending on the energy, skills, and judgment of the builders:

1. The simplest fort was an extra-large cabin surrounded by a stockade. Loopholes for firing rifles were cut into the stockade fence. An example of this is Figure 1, Trent's Fort at the forks of the Ohio (Pittsburgh). 3 This was built in 1754 and was there before the French established Ft. Duquesne. William Trent was a trader, not a farmer, and this fort was built to accommodate him and his men and not several farm families. Another illustration is (John) Harris's Fort, Figure 2, along the Susquehanna River at what is now Harrisburg. Harris was a farmer and also ran a ferry across the river. 4

2. A blockhouse. This structure would be two stories high, the first floor of which would be the primary home of the property owner and the second floor would be for incoming families and also serve as a high firing position for the defenders. Doddridge tells us that "Their upper stories were about eighteen inches every way larger in dimension than the under one, leaving an opening at the commencement of the second story to prevent the enemy from making a lodgment under their walls." 5

This overhang on the second floor has also been described as having an opening, or several openings, cut into the floor to enable one to fire downwards at Indians beating at the front door or at the windows. There is one story of women carrying pots of boiling water upstairs and pouring it down on Indians gathered around the door at the first level.

A picture of such a building is shown in Figures 3 and 4.

Figure I - This drawing shows the most primitive style of fort. It is taken from <u>Outposts of the War for the Empire</u> by Charles M. Stotz.

Figure 2

Harris' Fort

This is an artist's rendition of John Harris's fortified cabin along the Susquehanna River and was the beginning of present-say Harrisburg. (This is taken from *Frontier Forts of Pennsylvania, Vol. I.*)

This is the most basic type of settlers-fort. It lacked a second-story which would have increased vision and enabled defenders to fire down at their foe, and it had no stockade fence. In fact, a fence would have blocked the view of an attacking force.

This form or style of fort was not widely used in decidedly hostile country.

Figure 3 - A blockhouse - the staple of frontier defense. Above is the view from the outside and below is an interior view. It is from such a structure as this that Ann Hupp fought.

This drawing, and that on the next page, are by William Frankfort, an expert on frontier life.

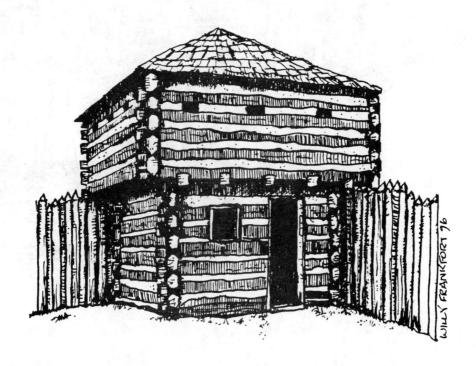

Figure 4 - This shows a cabin built into the stockade wall at a blockhouse. There would have been as many of these small dwellings as there were families to be accommodated - usually three or four.

WILLY FRANKFORT 96

One example of a kind of hybrid between a simple cabin and a two-story blockhouse is Stewart's Blockhouse. It's owner was the same Lazarus Stewart mentioned earlier in this book. He was a very tough man. This fort was built on the Susquehanna River in 1771. It was one and one-half stories high, had four rooms on the first floor and a large second floor for his neighbor-visitors and which also served as a good firing position.

"The part above the second floor projected beyond the walls of the first story; this overshoot, as it was called, enabled the occupants of the house to protect the walls from assault of an attacking party, in a manner as effective as from flanking towers." 6 See Figure 5.

Stewart's Blockhouse was attacked at least twice that we know of - once in June of 1781 when "The house was defended in great spirit, the women taking an active part in the defense," 7 and again on July 3rd and 4th of 1778. (Note - the frontier had moved far west, to the Ohio River, by 1778 but the Indians were still raiding in the center of the State). There may well have been other raids of which no record was made.

Those forts that were built in this manner were so identified, i.e., Miller's Blockhouse (where Ann Hupp fought), Reynold's Blockhouse and Stricker's Blockhouse, all of which have been located and are described in more detail in later pages.

3. A fort consisting of cabins, blockhouses and a stockade fence. This would be the largest type of frontier fort and Rev. Doddridge describes them:

"A range of cabins commonly formed one side, at least, of the fort. Divisions or partitions of logs separated the cabins from each other. The walls on the outside were ten or twelve feet high, the slope of the roof being turned wholly inward. A very few of these cabins had puncheon floors, the greater part were earthen. The blockhouses were built at the angles of the fort. They projected about two feet beyond the outer walls of the cabins and stockades. ....A large folding gate made of thick slabs, nearest the spring, closed the fort. The stockades, ...cabins and blockhouse walls, were furnished with portholes at proper heights and distances. The whole of the outside was made completely bullet proof.

It may truly be said that necessity is the mother of invention; for the whole of this work was made without the aid of a single nail or spike of iron, and for this reason, such things were not to be had." 8

Several of these large forts have been located - Lindley's, Cherry's, Vance's, Wolfe's, Doddridge's, Rice's and others - and pertinent information about them is set forth under their separate listings.

STEWART'S BLOCKHOUSE.

Figure 5

This drawing is based on a written description of the blockhouse. There was probably a stockade fence around this building.

This design is one step better than a fortified cabin, but the upper firing position appears to be more of a loft than a true second floor. It would not serve well as living quarters for gathering neighbors because of its small size and height. It would be adequate during a fight, but that is about all.

This drawing is taken from *Frontier Forts of Pennsylvania, Vol. I.*

Figure 6 - A "birds-eye" view of Pricketts Fort. Note the small cabins built into the stockade walls to house incoming families. Most forts would only have two, diagonal, blockhouses and would not have the two "community buildings" shown here. One is a meeting hall, the other a trading post and blacksmith's shop.

This drawing was prepared by William Frankfort

103

Figure 7

Prickett's Fort
Fairmont, WV

This is a perfect example of a frontier fort. The top photo shows the entrance, the stockade wall, and one blockhouse. There would be another blockhouse diagonally opposite this one. The Rev. Doddridge calls our attention to the fact that not one nail was used in the construction of these forts.

Close-up of blockhouse. Notice the firing ports and the fact that the upper story overhangs the lower story by 18 inches or so. Holes were cut in this "overhang" to enable settlers to fire down at Indians gathered close to the walls of the lower story.

Loopholes cut into the stockade fence. While some men (and women) fired from the two blockhouses, others would take position along the stockade wall and fire from there.

Figure 8

**Prickett's Fort
Fairmont, WV**

These forts would be 100 to 150 feet square and might contain six to ten of these tiny cabins. Everything depended on the number of families they served. The cabins are tiny - roughly 6 x 8 feet and contain two bunk beds. They were for the women and children; men and older boys slept outside. Note that the back wall of each cabin is the stockade fence and the inward sloping roofs were so fires from arrows or thrown torches could be put out without exposing the defenders. Also note the three-legged stools. The man and boy are dressed in period clothing. Try to imagine living in this compressed area for months at a time!

Figure 9

**Fort Steuben
Steubenville, OH**

This was a military fort, now being reconstructed on the original site. It measured 200 feet square and had a blockhouse at each of the four corners and a stockade fence. It was built in 1786 for the protection of government surveyors. The soldiers lived in the blockhouses and there were two small buildings for officer's quarters. It is bigger than any settler's fort, but is a good example of the construction and architecture of the time.

An excellent and wonderful reproduction of a large settlers-fort has been constructed in Fairmont, West Virginia and every reader of this book must visit Prickett's Fort State Park. Prickett's Fort is slightly larger than similar forts in this area but it fits Doddridge's description to a "T". A drawing and photographs that highlight some details are shown in Figures 6, 7, and 8.

For comparison purposes photographs of Fort Steuben in Steubenville, Ohio (also beautifully re-built) are shown in Figure 9. This was a military fort but it exemplifies the thought and planning of frontiers-people as they went about constructing a fort. The pictures help to identify the look of these places and will give you a sense of life in those times.

Returning to the description of Doddridge it is curious to note that he specifically mentions that the spring, for water, was often outside the gate: "...A large folding gate...nearest the spring, closed the fort." Clearly it would be best if the spring was inside the fort but sometimes this, apparently, was not possible. At Vance's Fort, Cox's Fort, and Rice's Fort the spring was outside the stockade walls. The builders must have had confidence that their rifles could cover anyone who had to make the short run to the spring and back. In retrospect that seems like one of those brilliant ideas that don't work out very well in practice. We are left ponder this question - with the fort under fire from Indians in the woods did the man (or men) who came up with this idea volunteer to go get the water? Or did he (they) suddenly become indispensable inside the fort and demand that someone else go?

To digress for a moment - that problem actually occurred in a hilarious incident at Bryant's Fort in Kentucky. There, the spring was located a short, but sizable, distance from the gate. We may guess, perhaps, one-hundred and fifty feet. A large war-party quietly set up an ambush in the woods near the gate and the spring. Then they sent a small number of their group to the other side of the fort to make a demonstration - yelling, whopping, firing their muskets. The thought was that the white men would rush out of the fort to attack the demonstrators and walk straight into the ambush. The settlers were completely surprised and, true to form, many young men wanted to leave the fort and attack those screaming, yelling Indians. More experienced people suspected a trap. They also surmised that a good ambush would likely be set up near the gate and the spring. It was decided that the wiser course was to stay in the fort. They had one serious problem - they had no water.

Now each morning the women would take various containers and troop to the spring to get water for their daily use and probably the Indians knew of this routine. The Indians always carefully studied places they were going to attack.

It was suggested therefore that the men would put on a demonstration of their own - shouting and yelling as if getting ready to charge from the fort. The women were asked to follow their daily schedule and go together to get the needed water. It was anticipated that the Indians would not expose their ambush by attacking the women but would let them pass in expectation of the men soon rushing from the fort.

Great plan. Good idea.

The women were outraged! They roared with indignation! "Go get your own water, you damned fools," they shouted. They were mad.

These were probably the kindest words used. They refused to budge.

It took the utmost exhortation of husband to wife and father to daughter - and the desperate need for water - before the women agreed.

They left, en masse, the safety of those solid wooden walls, mothers cautioning their young daughters to remain calm and walk slowly while gaily chatting. What an act they put on! They made it to the spring, quickly filled their containers with water (no one wanted to be last!) and then started the long stroll back, where every step was too slow and the gate an eternal distance away. We are told "...although their steps became quicker and quicker on their return, and when near the gate of the fort, degenerated into a rather unmilitary celerity, attended with some little crowding in passing the gate, yet not more than one-fifth of the water was spilled." The chronicler adds "... the eyes of the youngest had not dilated to more than double their ordinary size!" 9

Oh, for the life of a pioneer!

And so much for the idea of a spring outside the gates of the fort.

To finish the story, Bryant's Fort was besieged for several days and there was fierce fighting but the settlers held on and the Indians finally went away.

To return to our discussion of forts, there is an odd term used to describe some of them and that is the word "Station." It seems to have been used deliberately and in the same general area we find Millers Blockhouse, Rice's Fort, and Williamson's Station. We can clearly see the distinction between a blockhouse and a fort but the term "station" appears to be a word used, interchangeably, with "fort." It appears most often in reference to forts further down the Ohio River and in Kentucky. One knowledgeable author defines a "station" as :

> "A station was a parallelogram of cabins, united by palisades so as to present a continued wall on the outer side, the cabin doors opening into a common square on the inner side." 10

There is no mention of any blockhouse at the corners of this unit so perhaps that is the distinguishing feature between it and the "fort" of Doddridge.

Nowhere can there be found an accurate count of the numbers of forts (whatever the size or design) that were built in Western Pennsylvania. There is not even an estimate. They were so common - scattered about every few miles in a settled area - that, most likely, no one even thought of counting them. They ceased to be built after 1795 when the Indian raids stopped and they lost their utility. Most of them fell into disrepair and others were torn down so that the logs could be used for new cabins, corn-cribs, storage sheds, and the like. What does one do with an old two-story blockhouse?

A few numbers are available: "The building of frontier forts in the Revolution was one of the valuable lessons learned in the French (and Indian) war. There were erected during the campaigns of 1755-58 and that of 1763, no less than 207 forts, large and small. The chain formed two distinct barriers on the west. The outer one guarded what was the frontier against the French, along the east bank of the Ohio (and Allegheny) River, from Kittanning to the south-western corner of the province.

In addition to these forts, it became necessary at various points, where depredations were most frequent, to erect stockades around strongly-built farm houses and mills, or to build blockhouses specially as places of safety and defense." [11]

In later years, after the Great Land Rush of 1768 (the land purchase from the Iroquois) the building of such defensive structures seems to have become routine and there is a reference that "There were about one-hundred of these forts and blockhouses put up in the Revolutionary period west of the mountains." [12]

There is one other mention of numbers in a reference to forts constructed after the Revolution: "Fourteen blockhouses in Westmoreland, Armstrong, Allegheny, Indiana and Crawford counties were erected as protection against Indian attacks from the years 1783-1795." [13] This small number over such a wide area suggests that these were "government forts" and not private, settlers-forts.

We are left to conclude that there was never any attempt made to count the settler's forts and can only state that there were many of them.

Living in the Forts
"These were in the highest degree uncomfortable." [14]

That has to be the understatement of all time. If the fort had been built by four families, each consisting of husband, wife and five children, there was suddenly - in a matter of hours - twenty-eight persons of all ages crammed into a blockhouse, cabin, or small fort; and no one could venture outside the walls! To add to the problem these people often had to spend weeks, sometimes months, penned up in this tiny area. Talk about "cabin fever." The sanitation problems had to have been horrendous. What did they do with the garbage?

The settlers could expect Indian raids - and thus the necessity of living in the forts - from early Spring to the first snow-fall of late Autumn. How they looked forward to the first snow! Then they could be reasonably sure of safety in their own cabins. The most worrisome time of the year were those beautiful fall days we still call "Indian Summer." Today we have forgotten how those days of crisp mornings, warm afternoons, clear blue skies, and gorgeous orange and red foliage earned their fearsome designation. That was the time the Indians could be most expected to come raiding. Every fall there is a gorgeous full moon that we cheerfully refer to as a Harvest Moon. The frontiers people would look at that brilliant orange globe with its red splashes and mutter darkly to themselves and to each other "There's blood on the moon" reminding one and all that the time of most savage fighting and killing was at hand. Take a moment to think of that the next time you luxuriate in that beautiful Autumn weather. Things were different in the Olden Times.

That health problems developed because of this constricted, communal living is beyond question. With the Indians outside, and sickness inside, it must have been a terribly difficult time. One disconsolate father wrote:

"People in this country seem generally to have lost their health, but perhaps it is owing to the disagreeable way in which we are obliged to live crowded in forts, where the air seems to have lost all its purity and sweetness. Our poor little Billy has been exceedingly ill for several weeks and is reduced to a mere skeleton by a kind of flux which is common here and of which numbers die. His mother is almost disconsolate, and I myself are much afraid we shall lose the child; and if we do, I shall impute it to nothing but living in filth and dirt." [15]

Completely aside from the sanitation problems, the personality conflicts and "community relations" problems must have been equally bad. Granted that they were all neighbors and probably got along fairly well, still, how long can anyone - ourselves included

- live in intimate proximity to relatives and friends without nerves rubbing raw? Children will quarrel, women sharing one kitchen or cooking hearth do get in the way of each other, and men have differing opinions on many subjects. How must these things have been aggravated by being confined for days on end within the perimeter of the stockade walls. Armed men had to leave the fort from time to time to go on patrol looking for signs of Indians and there must have been many women who would have gladly volunteered for that hazardous duty. Anything to get out of that fort!

Surprisingly those persons who have left us reports on life in those days really don't mention quarrels or conflicts. Perhaps they were so ordinary, and expected, that they weren't worth mentioning or, maybe, we, in this distant time, tend to exaggerate them. Equally possible is the fact that the fear of attack and death at the hands of Indians was so strong that that, alone, calmed a lot of nerves and forced people to get along.

Rev. Doddridge does mention one "community problem" caused by some families and the resulting exasperation felt by the others when he tells us:

"Some families belonging to each fort were much less under the influence of fear than others, and who, after an alarm had subsided, in spite of every remonstrance, would remove home while their more prudent neighbors remained in the fort. Such families were denominated fool-hardy and gave no small amount of trouble by creating such frequent necessities of sending runners to warn them of their danger, and sometimes parties of our men to protect them during their removal." 16 (Emphasis supplied).

We can well imagine the anger and cursing that this sort of conduct evoked.

When there was no immediate danger the men did leave the fort and tried to work their fields under armed guard. This had to have been quite a clumsy and unsatisfactory arrangement - today we work in your field, tomorrow in mine, etc. - but these people were farmers and their crops were second in importance only to their lives.

"It was frequently the case that the settlers had to live in the forts for weeks at a time, taking their scanty house-hold goods, farm implements, and livestock with them into the enclosure. When there was no immediate danger outside, the men, leaving the women and children inside, went to their fields in the day and returned at night, but never without their rifles close at hand. Sentinels were placed at proper places, and on the least alarm the whole company of workers repaired to their arms." 17

That is a tough way to get any farming done. You can't handle a plow very well with a rifle on your back and a powder-horn hanging on your chest.

There were just endless problems caused by the Indian raids. The killing was bad enough but these people had to have food and the only way to get it was to grow it themselves, and you couldn't grow food with Indians around.

One weary soul poured out his heart with this doleful prediction:

"If there is not stors laid in this winter, in Spring they (the settlers) must leave the Country; they have no salt to Lay Up Meat, their Grain is all Burned and Destroyed on the North of the Cunnemach: if there is no store of Provisions for next Summer and People Hindered from Spring Crops, the Country is undoubtedly broke up." [18]

Oh, Pioneers! Would that we had a fraction of their courage and stamina.

They pleaded for help and rarely got it. Their pathetic letters went out to the Royal Governor, the Quaker Assembly, later to the Supreme Executive Council of Pennsylvania and still later to President George Washington. The letters are all the same:

"Sir: The dangerous situation that our frontiers at present seem to be in obliges us, your humble petitioners, to beg for your assistance at such a difficult time as it now is....We, the inhabitants...are...daily open to the rage of a savage and merciless enemy not withstanding the great care that they already been taken for our safety by placing guards on the river. The inhabitants that live near enough the mill to fort there look upon themselves not of sufficient force to guard the mill and carry on any labor to support their families. They will, therefore, undoubtedly break off, unless your excellency will please to grant them a few men to guard the mill." [19]

Help rarely came. They were on their own. They stuck it out, somehow.

But, they wouldn't leave.

NOTES

Six: THE FORTS

1. Thomas Lynch Montgomery (ed.), *Frontier Forts of Pennsylvania, Vol. II, 2d ed.* (Evensville, Ind.: Unigraphic, Inc., 1978, originally published 1916, Harrisburg, Pa.), p. 403.
2. Reuben Gold Thwaites and Louise Phelps Kellogg, Ed's, *Frontier Defense On The Upper Ohio, 1777-1778* (Madison, Wis.: Wisconsin Historical Society, 1912), p. 174, f.n. 38.
3. Charles Morse Stotz, *Outposts of the War for Empire* (Pittsburgh, Pa.: Historical Society of Western Pennsylvania, 1985), p. 90.
4. Thomas Lynch Montgomery (ed.), *Frontier Forts of Pennsylvania, Vol. I, 2d ed.* (Evensville, Ind.: Unigraphic, Inc., 1978, originally published 1916, Harrisburg, Pa.), p. 5.
5. Joseph Doddridge, *The Settlement and Indian Wars of the Western Parts of Virginia and Pennsylvania, 1763 - 1783* (Bowie, Maryland: Heritage Books, Inc., 1988; reprinted in 1912, Pittsburgh, Pa; originally published in 1824), p. 94.
6. Montgomery, ed., *Frontier Forts, Vol. 1*, pp. 450-451.
7. Ibid., p. 451.
8. Doddridge, p. 94.
9. I.D. Rupp, *Early History of Western Pennsylvania* (Lewisburg, PA: Wennawoods Publishing, 1995; originally published, 1846, Harrisburg, Pa.), pp. 243-244.
10. Montgomery, ed., *Frontier Forts, Vol. II*, p. 402.
11. Lewis S. Shimmell, *Border Warfare In Pennsylvania* (Harrisburg, Pa.: R.L. Myers & Company, 1901), p. 75.
12. Ibid., p. 77.
13. Ibid., p. 151.
14. Montgomery, ed., *Frontier Forts, Vol. II*, p. 403.
15. Louise Phelps Kellogg, ed., *Frontier Retreat on the Upper Ohio* (Bowie, Md., Heritage Books, Inc., 1994), pp. 186-187.
    This is a reprint of the original published in 1917 by the State Historical Society of Wisconsin.
16. Doddridge, pp. 95-96.
17. Shimmell, p. 76.
18. Ibid., p. 78.
19. Montgomery, ed., *Frontier Forts, Vol. II*, p. 421.

Chapter 7

The Individual Forts

A. Western Allegheny County and Northern Washington County

B. Monongahela River area; Tarentum

C. From the city of Washington west to the Ohio River - the Buffalo Creek Area

D. Western Washington County around the city of Avella

E. Southern Washington County; Greene County

A. <u>Western Allegheny County and Northern Washington County</u>

In the vicinities of:

Bethel Park - Canonsburg - Carnegie - McDonald - Midway - Burgettstown

The Robinson Run, Cherry Run, Raccoon Creek, and Chartiers Creek areas

Forts - East to West:

Couch, Froman, Ewing, McMichael, McDonald, Cherry, Beelor, Dillow, Burgett, Vance

Couch's Fort

This site has been precisely located.

Fort Couch Road intersects US Rt. 19 in Bethel park Borough nine miles south of Pittsburgh. The fort was located .6 miles south of that intersection at the present site of McDonald's Restaurant. A historical marker has been placed there by the Bethel Park Historical Society. The fort was in the valley on the east side of the road.

We are told in Cushing's <u>Genealogical History of Allegheny County</u> that Nathaniel Couch was with General Braddock in his 1755 expedition as a member of the Virginia Rifles under George Washington.

He was a lucky man to survive that fight because those Virginians not only had Indians to contend with, but many of them were killed by panicky British troops who fired on them because they were fighting from behind trees and rocks and the British soldiers mistook them for Indians.

It is believed that Couch came here to stay in 1769-1770. He built the fort at that time when there were numerous Indian raids in this general area. On April 3 1780, he entered a claim for 400 acres of land with the Virginia Land Office. His property was surveyed February 7, 1786, on a Virginia Certificate but he received his deed (Patent) from Pennsylvania on April 7, 1788, for 366 acres and 72 perches. He paid three pounds and ten pence for the land and called it "Titlenure," an odd name that has no significance today.

The old structure seems to have survived until it was torn down in 1890. On the foundation was built the Fort Couch Inn in 1927, later the Pioneer Inn, and the chimney and fireplace were incorporated into that new building. In turn the Pioneer Inn was torn down several years ago when McDonald's was constructed and nothing now remains of the old fort.

Nothing is known about activities at this fort until the Whiskey Rebellion of 1794. It must have been a well-known meeting place and may have had a tavern because rebel meetings were held here and no such gathering was complete without whiskey. The angry farmers met to plan their attack on the house of Gen. Neville, the chief tax collector, and returned here after that attack. Nearly 500 men were involved in the assault which was successful (the house was burned) and when the insurgents returned to Couch's Fort they were undoubtedly thirsty and ready to celebrate.

Much historical material is maintained at the nearby Bethel Presbyterian Church (Couch sold an acre of his land for the establishment of the church) and the fort is mentioned in all accounts of the Whiskey Rebellion.

Couch's Fort

This historical marker was placed by the Bethel Park Historical Society.

This view looks west along Fort Couch Road. The fort was in the valley, on the north side of the road, at the "Golden Arches" sign for McDonald's restaurant.

The restaurant is located at the site of the fort. A stream flows to the rear of these buildings.

Froman's Fort

The location of this fort is in the category of "highly probable" but not positive. It is in North Strabane Township, Washington County, just a few miles south of Canonsburg and very near the Allegheny County line.

To reach this spot from the Pittsburgh area proceed down US Rt. 19 S to the Hill Church cloverleaf and there get on State Rt. 519 going south. Proceed 3 miles, past the North Strabane municipal building, and to an "S" curve over an old concrete bridge over Linden Creek. The fort site is in the meadow to your right (west). For further identification there is the presence of Thistledown Farm on the hill, south of the meadow, and about 300 yards from the bridge.

The fort is believed to have been located in the meadow beside the creek. In the same area Paul Froman had a grist mill.

Dr. Jim Herron was a very well known local historian and he grew up in this area. He pointed out the spot to Mr. Harold Cypher who advised me of the location. Unfortunately there is no documentary support for this location.

In both Frontier Forts of Pennsylvania and The History of Washington County by Forrest, this fort is placed in the present city of Canonsburg along Chartiers Creek. Those authors either didn't know, or disregarded, the fact that Linden Creek was once known as Chartiers Creek, and that before Canonsburg came to be there was a substantial settlement in the vicinity of the present village of Linden known as "Shirtee's Settlement." The land of Paul Froman was located there. The creek was known as "Chartee's Creek" and "Shirtee's Creek."

There is a deed dated September 9, 1777, conveying land in "Shirtee's Settlement" from Michael Thomas and Thomas Cook to the Rev. John McMillan and it is along "Shirtee's Creek" and bounded on the south by land of Paul Froman.

Paul Froman was clearly here before 1777, and he owned about 1700 acres of land. He was a leading citizen of the time and most of the roads in the area focused on his mill or the nearby village of Linden. Thus a road was established from "Thomas Gist's to Paul Froman's Mill on Shirtee's Creek" and another from Redstone Old Fort (Brownsville) to Froman's Mill. There was even talk of making Linden the county seat if, and when, a new county was formed.

This and other information is set forth in a pamphlet published to celebrate the Centennial of Canonsburg (1802 - 1902).

Froman was a Militia Captain and was named a member of the Board of Viewers who were public officials involved in real estate matters and the laying out of roads.

We know very little about this fort. An Indian scout for the white people, known as Capt. Whiteyes, reported his cabin was robbed by some Virginians and about 30 pounds worth of property taken which he learned was "divided and sold by the robbers at one Froman's Fort, on Chartiers Creek."

Beyond this reference, nothing more is known.

Froman's Fort

This shows the road (Rt. 519) coming south and over the bridge over Linden Creek. The fort was in the meadow to the left. The grist mill was probably also there or very close by. Linden Creek (formerly Shirtees or Chartiers Creek) flows along the far left, then turns and comes across the back of the meadow, under the bridge, then turns again and come down along the right side of the road.

Ewing's Fort

The location of this fort has been accurately determined. It is just about 3/4 of a mile west of the borough of Carnegie in Allegheny County along Old Noblestown Road.

The construction of Interstate 79 and the Carnegie Interchange obliterated some old landmarks, bisected Noblestown Road, and changed the course of a part of Robinson Run, but while difficult, the site can still be found.

Proceed on Interstate 79 to the Carnegie interchange and there turn off onto Noblestown Road heading west. Follow this for .5 miles and then turn right (north) onto Old Noblestown Road. After two hundred feet this road swings to the right (east) and proceeds 100 feet to a "Y." Take the left arm of the "Y" (still Old Noblestown Road) and go on past the large Polar Water Company complex, for .5 miles to the fort site. The road makes a 90° turn at this point and the fort was at the angle of the turn. As you will see it lies at the base of the hill which carries I-79 at the top. This area is known as Lick Hollow.

Explicit directions were given in a June, 1952, volume of the Western Pennsylvania Historical Society Magazine at Pp. 96-97, but due to the new construction the old landmarks are hard to find. Mr. Bill Lane, whose business, Lane Block Company, is nearby, took us to this site. He states that there was an old log cabin, a part of the fort complex, at this site which he, and others, made an effort to preserve, but to no avail. The interstate construction required its destruction.

James Ewing came into this area in 1770 and years later, became the first Recorder of Allegheny County. He secured two parcels of land, the most easterly being 378 acres surveyed May 27, 1785, and patented on a Virginia Certificate dated April 18, 1788. This he called "Mill Mount" and is the portion upon which the fort was built. The second lot, to the west, was of 300 acres and the warrant is dated February 10, 1785. The property extended through present Eldersville to present Walker's Mill.

Isaac Walker and his brother Gabriel Walker came here two years later and settled west of Ewing.

The terrible tragedy that befell the Gabriel Walker family in 1782 is recounted elsewhere but it is to Ewing's Fort that the survivors ran, including Mrs. Walker with her infant baby and toddler. They ran for four miles to get here. It was in the fields surrounding this fort that the two Walker boys were murdered by the Indians. The men who left here to trail the

Indians included Captain Casnes, John Henry, James Ewing, Peter Hickman, John Connors, and Gabriel Walker.

Nothing more is known about activities at this fort.

Ewing's Fort

This view looks east along Old Noblestown Road. The fort site is on the left at the 90° turn of the road. The hillside supports I-79 at its top. Highway construction destroyed or altered the actual location.

Thick vegetation covers the site and only a few feet into this brush the steep hillside begins.

This shows the fields south of the fort site. Robinson Run is to the right. It is possible that it is in this field that the two Walker boys were murdered by Indians.

McMichal's Blockhouse

The location of this fort is reasonably certain. The site is confirmed by Mr. William Vogel who is a McMichael heir and a Senior Citizen. His grandmother, Florence (McMichael) Sturgeon pointed out the spot to him on many occasions and discussed the existence of the blockhouse. More recently his niece, Mrs. Carol DePaul, also a McMichael heir, has done some studies which confirm the fact.

This blockhouse was located in Robinson Township, Allegheny County, near the northeasterly edge of present Settler's Cabin County Park. It is on the southwesterly corner of the intersection of Ridge Road and McMichael Road.

To get to this site proceed on I-79 to the Carnegie Interchange. Turn off there and go west on Noblestown Road 1.9 miles to McMichael Road. Turn right (north) on McMichael Road for 2.5 miles to its intersection with Ridge Road. The blockhouse stood on the top of the slight hill to your left (west).

As a point of interest there stands an old log cabin on McMichael Road .8 miles north of Noblestown Road on the left (west) side of the road.

John McMichael and his wife, Nancy, came from Maryland around 1774, and he is identified as a farmer and surveyor. He claimed 800 acres of land. From June 14, 1782, to September 15, 1782, he served as a Private in the Washington County Militia under Captain Joseph Cessna.

A pension application by John Kincaid shows that on April 1, 1779, he was drafted for a six months tour of duty, and he "marched to McMichael's Fort where the company was under the command of Col. Cox." Apparently a militia company was stationed there at that time.

Another pension application, that for Henry Shaffer, shows that in 1779 he served a total of seven months militia duty in Captain Zadock Wright's company "at McMichael Station."

Little more is known about this fort and nothing about events that may have occurred there.

McMichael's Blockhouse

The fort stood on a plateau behind the trees at this intersection of McMichael Road (left) and Ridge Road (right).

This is from the fort site looking down on McMichael Road. The intersection is to the left.

This Walker-Ewing log cabin, on McMichael Road, 1.7 miles east of the fort site, was built about 1790.

McDonald's Fort

The location of this fort has some problems - there are two possible sites which are .4 miles apart and both on property known to have been owned by John McDonald.

McDonald came into this area in 1773 and took up a tract of land of 1000 acres which he called "Mt. Pleasant." Shortly thereafter he purchased another 1000 acres on the westerly side of "Mt. Pleasant" and near the present village of Primrose.

To reach these sites proceed to the town of McDonald. In the center of town there is a traffic light. At this light get on to State Rt. 980 N (Noblestown Road) and proceed for .3 miles. On the right (north) side of the road is a large and beautiful white house at 8018 Noblestown Road, the home of Mr. and Mrs. Kim Darragh. Mr. Darragh was a prominent attorney in Pittsburgh, now retired. The house is situated on a plateau rising about thirty feet above the road. Robinson Run lies about two hundred yards to the south. This is Site No. 1.

From this location continue westwardly on Noblestown Road. (Note: Route 980N turns right (north) shortly beyond the Darragh house and do not follow that road; proceed directly west on Noblestown Road). Continue westward for .4 miles from the Darragh home to Cooks Road. Turn right (north) on to Cooks Road and then immediately left onto a gravel drive which goes directly to the lovely red-brick home of Mr. and Mrs. Earl Ray Petrucci, 8606 Noblestown Road. This home is also located on a plateau above the road. Robinson Run is about 150 yards to the south, and on the east side of the house, perhaps 50 yards away, there is a small stream coming from the north which goes into Robinson Run. This is Site No. 2.

Mr. A.D. White, a prominent historian, wrote in his "Historical Sketches of Northern Washington County" that the fort was at the Darragh home, Site 1.

Mrs. Erma Novak has lived in McDonald all of her life and is an expert on McDonald history, and she advises that it was at the Petrucci home, Site 2.

The Petrucci home was built in the 1830's by a grandson of John McDonald. To the rear of the house, about 50 feet north, stands a small log structure about 10 feet square and obviously old. Photographs of it were submitted to Mr. Bruce Bomberger, architectural services section , Pennsylvania Historical and Museum Commission, for analysis, and he states that "it was probably built sometime during the period from the late 18th through the first several decades of the 19th centuries."

John McDonald served as a Justice of the Peace and was an Indian trader and he had buildings for these purposes. Could this small log building have been a storage place for furs taken in trade with the Indians?

There is an interesting petition, dated April 5, 1782, and directed to General Irvine "commandant on the western waters." It is signed by John McDonald and nine other men. They had met that day at the house of John McDonald and advise that they have "lived in a state of anarchy since 1777;" that "we expect nothing else but that the Indians will be immediately amongst us;" that they are determined to make a stand there that summer and request ten men as a garrison plus rifles, powder, and lead. They extol the virtues of the fort and agree to store the supplies at no cost to the state:

"The situation of McDonald's place is pleasant, lying and being on a knoll or advantageous piece of ground for any garrison. We, the subscribers, observing that the states must have receiving and issuing stores, it is our opinion that according to McDonald's promise, we think it the best place for said stores. McDonald's promises are that the states shall have, without cost, his still-house, hogsheads, his cellar under his new house, together with the lowest story of his spring-house, without price or fee to the states."

Apparently they got the men because there is a record of the Supreme Executive Council of Pennsylvania dated February 18, 1790, approving payment "of Joseph Brown for one month's pay as a volunteer militia man, while stationed at one McDonald's, for the defense of the county of Washington, in Aug., 1782, amounting to five pounds, five shillings." (Poor Mr. Brown had to wait eight years for his money!)

A man named Spencer Records wrote a narrative of his life and he recalls that his family "forted" at McDonald's in 1778 and again from 1780 to 1782 when there were the "usual alarms and excursions on the Pennsylvania frontier."

We may fairly conclude that McDonald's Fort was a veritable bee-hive of activity between settlers "forting" there, soldiers stationed there, and John McDonald acting as both a Justice of the Peace and an Indian trader. To add to the excitement throw in eleven children - the progeny of John and his wife, Martha. It was a lively place.

McDonald's Fort
Site 1

This lovely home marks one site declared by some authorities to be the location of the fort. As the second photo shows, it sits on a large plateau which would have been required for a big fort. The third picture shows a good, level area for farming with Robinson Run at the tree line.

McDonald's Fort
Site 2

This beautiful home was built in the 1830's by the grandson of John McDonald. It sits on a broad plateau overlooking Robinson Run.

This old log structure, to the rear of the house, was built between 1780 and 1820. McDonald was an Indian trader. Could this have been used to store furs?

Detail of the construction style used in building this structure.

Cherry's Fort

The site of this fort has been located through the help of Mr. Ray Johnson, Principal of Ft. Cherry High School and a local historian. It is in Mount Pleasant Township, Washington County on Cherry Valley Road.

To get there proceed on State Rt. 50 W to the village of Hickory. On the east side of Hickory turn right (north) on Ft. Cherry Road and go on for three miles to its intersection with Cherry Valley Road. Turn left (west) onto Cherry Valley Road and travel for 1.3 miles to the site. It is on the right (north) side of the road at a white house presently occupied by the Robert Cook family. As a further check, note that one hundred feet further west Beechnut Road enters from the left (south).

The original spring is along the side of the road directly in front of the house.

This was a very large, very well-known fort. It consisted of three log buildings, one twenty-five feet square, the others a little smaller. They were arranged in a triangular form and a stockade fence surrounded them. The large building was of two stories with a half-story above that served as a kind of "lookout." Of those who "forted" here we are sure of only two families, the McCarthys and the Rankins.

It is interesting to note that two other large forts were relatively close by - Beelor's Fort about three miles north and McDonald's Fort three miles east.

This fort was built in the summer of 1774 by Thomas Cherry who came here from Maryland. Shortly after building the fort poor Thomas was found dead at the spring. The fact that his gun was empty, that he had been killed by a bullet, and that he was not scalped led people to believe that it was an accident occurring while he was getting a drink of water. He was the first person buried in the cemetery which lay beyond the fort to the north.

It was to Cherry's Fort that the young Jackson boy ran to announce the capture of his father by Indians. Here, Andrew Poe organized the party who went in pursuit and which led to his famous battle with Dakadulah, previously recounted. John Cherry, son of Thomas, was in the party, fired the first shot at the Indians, and was killed in the return fire.

The fact that Andrew Poe was able to get the rescuing party together so quickly leads to a belief that militia men were stationed here. This fort had a reputation as a center for social and religious activities in the area.

Cherry's Fort

This view is taken from the west side of the house now standing at the fort site along Cherry Valley Road. This was a very large and strong fort consisting of three log buildings and a stockade.

This looks to the north. The cemetery was located near or among the trees in the rear of the fort.

This is believed to be the original spring, now along the road. Thomas Cherry was found, shot and dead, at this spot.

Beelor's Fort

The location of this fort has been accurately determined. It is in the village of Candor, Robinson Township, Washington County, about three miles north of the town of Midway and five miles east of Burgettstown.

To get to this location from Pittsburgh go out the Parkway West and swing onto US Rt. 22 W, and proceed for 7.4 miles to State Rt. 980 (McDonald-Midway). Take 980 S for 1.8 miles to Beech-Hollow Road. Turn right (west) and proceed on this road 1.4 miles to Candor Road. Turn left (south) and go .4 miles to Candor and the driveway of the Raccoon Presbyterian Church (established in 1778). The fort site is the small house 100 yards southwest of the church sitting on a plateau of land.

Captain Sam Beelor was the first white man into this area along Raccoon Creek, arriving here in 1774. He applied to Virginia for a Certificate on 400 acres with "preemption rights" on an additional 1000 acres. It was surveyed on March 17, 1782 and recorded in Virginia on July 17, 1782.

It is very interesting to note that this legal work was not good enough in the case of Sam Beelor - Virginia had given up its claim to this land by that time. He had to do it all over again according to Pennsylvania laws, but the authorities pretty much agreed with Virginia so Beelor received his patent (deed) for 400 acres which he called "Big Levels."

Sam Jr. came with his father and secured an adjoining piece of land as did Alexander Dunlap and his son, John. These were the first four families to take up residence here.

The Beelor Fort was quickly constructed to protect these people, and it is described as a two-story structure "large and strong." There was probably a stockade fence around it. It became a center for social and religious activities in the area. An early survey shows one trail running northeastwardly "To Turners Fort" and another trail labeled "To Dillow's Fort." In 1783 there was a petition filed asking for a road from Well's Fort and Mill (near Avella) to Beelor's Fort.

The Reverend John McMillan, a prominent minister of this time, notes in his journal that in December, 1778, he preached "at Raccoon" and in June, 1779, "at Beelor's place on Raccoon."

The private records of the Shane family reveal that in 1790 Timothy Shane and his wife, Hannah, outran an Indian raiding party to get to Beelor's Fort, and that while the Indians were attacking it Hannah gave birth to their son, John.

The McDonalds tell the same kind of story - before they built McDonalds Fort, and while her husband was gone, Martha McDonald was given the dreaded word that Indians were around and to get to a fort quickly. She rode five miles to Beelor's and a few hours later give birth to twin boys - Andrew and William.

The place was practically a maternity hospital!

There were many sad stories too.

The McKinleys lived nearby and two boys were attacked and killed by Indians as they tended their horses.

In July, 1780, William Bailey, two sons of William McCandless, and a Mr. McNeely were helping Robert Shearer, Jr. harvest wheat. At one point they stopped to rest. Bailey sat on a stump while the others went to a nearby stream for a cool, refreshing drink of water. It was to be their last drink. Indians attacked and killed all four of them. Bailey ran, but in jumping a gully he slipped on the far bank and the Indians captured him and headed for the Ohio River. Word of the killings reached Beelor's Fort where a party of men soon gathered and started following the trail. They reached the river just as the Indians were shoving off in their canoes. William Bailey was seated in a canoe, his wrists bound behind his back, with one Indian. The settlers opened fire and killed the Indian who was paddling Bailey's canoe, but as that warrior fell into the water he tipped the canoe and over it went. The rescuers had to dive into the river and swim to Bailey, but they reached him and dragged him to shore safely.

These stories, of hair-breath rescue, are just amazing. Sadly, many times they were the exception, not the rule.

The Shearers were very unlucky. They had lost Robert, Jr. in that raid. Now, sometime later, Robert, Sr. and another son, Hugh, were working in a field and were attacked. Hugh was killed and Robert, Sr. was taken prisoner. He remained with the Indians for eleven months, then escaped and returned home.

Sam Brady and his Rangers followed a Wyandot war-party of 12 to 14 men headed for Beelor's Fort. Brady set up an ambush to meet them on their return. The Indians attacked the fort shortly after dawn of September 30, 1779, and in the next two hours of fighting killed four people. They captured three men who had gone out into the fields to work. Then they broke off the attack and headed for the Ohio River with their prisoners. Brady and his Rangers were there to greet them, and in a sharp fight most of the Wyandots were killed and the three prisoners were re-taken safely.

There were many small fights around this fort. On August 2, 1780, Timothy Shane and Alexander Wright were patrolling about one-half mile from the fort when they heard shots fired nearby and, upon investigation, found evidence of a war-party. They killed one Indian then raced to the fort to give the alarm.

This was just another day on the western Pennsylvania frontier.

On April 27, 1781, some 53 volunteers - called "six months men" for their term of service - arrived at the fort, and, there, were split up into small groups and sent to various forts in the area to help protect them and, most importantly, to patrol the neighborhoods.

Beelor's Fort

This fort was located at the site of the house in the center of these pictures.

The raccoon Presbyterian Church is 100 yards east of the fort site. The present building is at the same place occupied by the original church which was built while the fort was in existence.

Dillow's Fort

The site of this fort has been accurately located with the help of Mrs. Jean (Armor) Stout who is a descendent of Thomas Armor, one of the original settlers in this area. Mrs. Stout lives on a portion of the original Armor grant near the village of Clinton.

To get to this location from the Pittsburgh area, proceed out the Parkway West to the 22/30 Interchange and turn off onto US 22 and 30 W headed toward Steubenville and Weirton. After about one mile US Rt. 30 W cuts off to the right. Turn onto Rt. 30 at this point and proceed for 7.1 miles to a "Y" in the road. Rt. 30 will curve to the right and the road to the left will be the Clinton-Frankfort Road. Follow the Clinton-Frankfort Road for 3.8 miles to Haul Road which comes up from the left. Turn left (south) on Haul Road and go .6 miles to Dilloe Road. Turn left (east) on Dilloe Road and go .2 miles. The fort was on a plateau on the right (north) side of this road about 1/4 of the way up the hill.

There was a one-room country school (known as Dillow School) built on the foundation of the fort, and Mrs. Jean Stout attended that school in her childhood. Careful study will reveal the faint trace of road tracks leading from Dillow Road to the location of the school (and fort). Those tracks go diagonally up the hill about two hundred feet. Pieces of old lumber can be seen, strewn about, that may be remains of the school.

Dillow Run, which leads into Raccoon Creek, is in the valley about 200 feet from the fort site.

This land is in Hanover Township, Washington County.

Michael Dillow settled here sometime before 1780. The tract of 399 acres was called "Dillows Fort" and a Virginia Certificate was issued on March 21, 1780. Michael Dillow didn't live long enough to get the deed. It's an old story - in 1782, exact date unknown, he and his son were working in a field when Indians killed him and took his son prisoner. The son saw the Indians throw his father's body alongside the trunk of a fallen tree. The boy was kept prisoner for several years and either escaped or was released. He came home and led his neighbors in a search for his father's remains. The bones were found beside the tree trunk, and the son saw to the proper burial of his father.

The land of Thomas Armor adjoined that of Dillow and not far away, on Raccoon Creek, was that of William Anderson. In July, 1779, William Anderson was shot from ambush and wounded but managed to get to the cabin of Armor. Tom Armor was a man of great strength, and he put Anderson on his back and carried him two miles to Dillow's Fort.

In the meantime Mrs. Anderson had heard the shot, grabbed her baby and raced from the cabin into the woods. She left behind two boys, aged four and seven years, who apparently were playing outside. The Indians captured the boys, ransacked the cabin, set it afire, and then searched for Mrs. Anderson. They couldn't find her and, eventually, left. The little boys were never heard from again.

General Broadhead, at Ft. Pitt, reported this incident in a letter dated August 1, 1779:

"I have just received information that one Anderson, who lived about two miles from Dillar's (Dillow's) Fort, was slightly wounded, and two of his little boys carried off by the savages on the same day the mischief was done in Wheeling."

The raiding was still going on thirteen years later. On February 13, 1792, Col. Redick writes to the Governor about the defensive posture of the settlements:

"...I find that a considerable gap is left open to the enemy on the northwesterly part of the county, and that a place where, in former wars the enemy perpetually made their approach on that quarter - the settlements on Raccoon, especially about Dilloe's constantly experienced in former times the repeated attacks of the enemy." (Emphasis Supplied)

I think we can conclude that Dillow's Fort was well used.

Dillow's Fort

The fort site on the north side of Dilloe Road and into the woods about fifty feet.

Decaying lumber and debris at the site. This is probably remnants of the one-room Dillow School that was built on the foundation.

This view, looking west, from the site, along Dilloe Road.

Burgett's Fort

The site of this fort has been accurately located by the members of the Ft. Vance Historical Society located in Burgettstown, Washington County. The fort was situated in the middle of town, on a plateau above the road, on the east side of State Rt. 18 (Main Street), almost directly opposite Our Lady of Lourdes Catholic Church. A small stone monument, placed there by the historical society, marks the location. There are four stone steps on the hillside believed to be original steps.

Sebastian Burgett was a German immigrant who came into this area in 1780 and secured a Virginia Patent on two tracts of land - one of 329 acres (where the fort was erected) he called "West Boston" and another, to the west, of 297 acres he called "Radius." (Where in the world did they get these names?) He built a grist mill near the fort on Little Raccoon Creek.

It is interesting to trace the movements of this man and his family. When he first arrived from Germany he settled with his wife and three children in Berks County in the eastern part of the state. His wife died and he then moved in 1773 to the vicinity of what is now West Newton in Westmoreland County. Here he met and married Roxana Markle. He apparently lived there about seven years then moved farther west to this Burgettstown area.

We can't help but to wonder why he kept moving.

Sebastian was killed in a accident on September 4, 1781. He was bringing a load of castings from Pittsburgh for his grist mill when the wagon tipped over and he was crushed under the load.

The old building stood for many years until, finally, one Boston Burgett decided that he wanted to build a new house on the site. He tore down the old log structure and used it to build a small barn across the street. He reported that bullet holes and tomahawk marks were visible on some of the logs. The bullet marks would certainly indicate hostile action but the so-called tomahawk marks were most likely made by a member of the family, or someone else, who temporarily imbedded a tomahawk in the log to secure it while he, or she, went on with other chores. It is hard to imagine an attacking Indian doing this for any reason.

Beyond this we know nothing about the shape or design of the fort, nor of any activities that occurred around it.

Burgett's Fort

This site is in the middle of Burgettstown and across the street from Our Lady of Lourdes Catholic Church. The stone steps, shown in the foreground of the bottom picture, are believed to be original steps utilized at the fort site.

SITE OF
BURGETT HOME AND FORT
CIRCA
1780

Vance's Fort

This was one of the most famous forts in this part of the frontier and it was a large one. As many as twenty-five families took refuge here and stayed for long periods of time.

The site of this fort has been accurately located by the Ft. Vance Historical Society and a marker has been placed at the location. It is on the farm of the Rommes family just outside of Burgettstown.

To get there drive to Burgettstown on State Rt. 18 N. In the middle of town, just north of Our Lady of Lourdes Catholic Church, turn left (west) onto Market Street. Within 300 feet this becomes Langeloth Road. Proceed onward for .9 miles to Vance Road which enters from the left (south). A distinctive marker at this point is a very high, red and white painted industrial smoke stack. Turn left (south) on Vance Road and proceed for 1.2 miles. Rommes farm lane of dirt and gravel will be on the left (east) side of the road. Go down this lane to the end, .3 miles, to the barn. The fort site is on the left, to the north of the barn about one hundred feet. An historical marker is at the spot. The spring is located near to the barn and about 100 feet south of the marker. Note that this is one of those forts in which the spring is located outside of the gate.

Joseph Vance, of Scotch-Irish descent, came here in 1774 from Winchester, Virginia. Numerous other settlers arrived at the same time, some directly from Scotland and Ireland, others from around York, Pennsylvania, Winchester, Virginia, and Mecklenburg, North Carolina. Most of them "forted" at Vance's Fort.

There are numerous stories about activities at and around this fort. The first sermon preached in this area was delivered by the Reverend James Powers on September 14, 1778. He stood under an oak tree just beyond the walls of the fort with his congregation gathered around him.

Joseph Vance, and others, gathered here to formulate their plans for the attack on the Indian village at Gnaddenhutten which resulted in the infamous Moravian Massacre.

A girl was killed by Indians right at the spring while she was filling her bucket with water, and William Parks was killed and scalped within sight of the fort as he was running to it.

Mrs. Meek was a noted midwife in this area, and a man rode from the fort one night to get her to assist in a delivery. In the early dawn they were seen and chased by Indians, one of whom got close enough to Mrs. Meek that he hurled his tomahawk at her. It missed, but hit a nearby tree slicing off the bark which hit Mrs. Meek in the face giving her a severe laceration. She and her companion made it to the fort. We aren't told whether the baby was a boy or a girl.

One heartwarming story relates to the serious economic troubles of the time. Joseph Vance became an Elder of the Cross Creek Presbyterian Church and its pastor was paid by the congregation. In 1787 the people had a poor market for their crops and were suffering. Among other things they couldn't pay their minister and were in danger of losing him. The idea was conceived to grind their wheat into flour and to take it all the way to New Orleans for sale. Everyone got together, ground their wheat into flour, secured a flatboat, loaded it, and William Smiley, an Elder of the church, together with Archibald Allison and John McClean, two adventurous young men, headed down river from Wellsburg, West Virginia, for New Orleans. They were gone for nine months and were given up for lost when one day they miraculously reappeared. At a congregational meeting they dumped onto a table, from a large bag, more gold coins than anyone had ever seen or ever dreamed of seeing. That was a second miracle. The flour had sold for $27.00 a barrel - an unheard of price. There was enough money to pay all arrearages to the pastor plus a year's salary in advance, three hundred dollars to Elder Smiley, one hundred dollars each to his two young assistants, enough to pay each parishioner for the flour he sent on the trip, and then a "dividend" to every parishioner.

The real miracle was that Smiley and his small crew actually made it to New Orleans and then back home with all that money. They successfully avoided accidents, Indians, and thieves on that 2000 mile journey. It was an almost unbelievable adventure.

Mrs. Wallace whose capture and later killing actually instigated the Gnaddenutten affair lived about five miles north of this fort. When she was discovered missing, with her baby, Mr. Wallace raced to this fort to seek assistance in following the Indians to try to rescue his wife and baby.

We can be reasonably certain that it looked very much like the photographs of Prickett's Fort.

Vance's Fort

The fort was located just to the left of the small building on the left side of the road.

This shows the marker that has been placed at the site. The spring was to the right side of the line of trees in the background. It was outside of the stockade fence that surrounded the fort.

The photo more precisely shows the fort location although it was a large one and occupied a good portion of this land.

B. Monongahela River Area; Tarentum

in the vicinities of:

White Oak - Large - Gastonville - Tarentum

Forts:

Reburn, Field, Cox, Bull Creek

Reburn's Fort

The site of this fort has been located, and a historical marker placed, by the Alliquippa Chapter of the Daughters of the American Revolution. It is in the Borough of White Oak, Allegheny County, close to McKeesport.

To get there from Pittsburgh get on US Rt. 30 and proceed eastwardly about six miles to its intersection with State Rt. 48 which comes from the right (south). From this intersection continue on US 30 for 1.7 miles to Muse Lane (presently not marked with a street sign). Turn right (south) on Muse Lane and proceed for 1.1 miles to the historical marker at the entrance to Angora Gardens in White Oak Regional Park.

This fort was a blockhouse built by Adam Reburn in 1788 on a part of the 266 acres he patented under the biblical name "Galilee."

There is a story that two brothers of John Noel were on their way to visit him when they were ambushed and killed by Indians and were buried near Noels Run close by the blockhouse.

A confirmed tale of the times is one involving two daughters of Adam Reburn and their cousin, Robert Couzens. In June of 1779 or 1780 they were working in a nearby corn field when they were attacked by Indians. Robert was killed but the girls ran for the blockhouse and arrived safely. Adam is reported as blowing on a conch shell to alert the neighbors and to summon help. A group of men did come to the blockhouse, a pursuit party was organized and set off after the Indians, but they had withdrawn and their trail could not be found.

Nothing further is known about activities at this fort.

Reburn's Fort

The historical marker placed in 1972 by McKeesport's Queen Alliquippa Chapter of the Daughters of the American Revolution.

FORT REBURN

Original site of a blockhouse built by area settlers as protection from Indians. The patent was acquired in 1786 by one of the builders, Adam Reburn, and became known as "Fort Reburn." Reburn's 218¼-acre homestead, "Galilee," was purchased in 1834 by John Jones Muse, Esq. in whose family it remained until it became part of the Allegheny Regional Parks System in 1967. Muse was the son of Fauntleroy Muse, Lieutenant of the Indian Wars and soldier of the American Revolution.

This is from Muse Lane looking north toward the marker. There is a natural gully not too far behind the marker so it is most likely the blockhouse was more to the left.

This old house is a part of Angora Gardens. The blockhouse site would, most likely, have been in this side-yard of the house.

Fort Field

The location of this fort is in the "highly probable" category, but there is a disturbing comment in an early record which raises some doubts.

The site is located in the village of Large, Jefferson Borough, Allegheny County. To find it proceed south on State Rt. 51 into Large. On the right (west) side of the road is a school building, and that was the site of the fort. The school is now abandoned but was known as Roosevelt School. For identification purposes, it is just north of the office building for Dick Corporation. It is exactly at the junction of Lewis Run and Peters Creek.

When the school building was constructed in 1937 corner posts of the old fort were uncovered and numerous artifacts were found.

The disquieting note is sounded by Mr. Noah Thompson, a respected local historian, who wrote a pamphlet entitled "Early History of the Peters Creek Valley and the Early Settlers." He places the fort in this area, but then adds (from some unknown source) "It was only accessible from one point being a natural fortification and afforded a view of nearly eight miles up and down the creek." There is no position anywhere in the entire area that affords a view of eight miles and no hill nearby has a position such that it is accessible from only one point. This description has to be in error.

The first settler in this area was Zaddock Wright, who had served in Braddock's Expedition, and came here around 1774 claming 440 acres on a Virginia Certificate known as "Wrightsburg." It is on this land that the fort was built. It is interesting that the fort was not named after the landowner as all of the others were. Apparently it was referred to as the "fort down in the field" which was shortened in due course to "Fort Field."

Adjacent to the school building, and to the north , is the Large Hotel, a very old structure in excellent condition today. This was built on land owned by "Frenchman" Ferree, and it is possible that he owned the land upon which the fort was located.

That Indian raids occurred here is evident by the fact that a Ranger group called "The Peters Creek Rangers" existed and was active in this area.

There seems to have been a well-used trail that ran through this valley, today's Rt. 51 follows it, passing directly in front of Fort Field. There is a report that as far back as 1754 Ensign Edward Ward and forty-one men passed along this trail going from the vicinity of Fort Pitt back to Virginia. It may be recalled that he and his men had been sent by Virginia to construct a fort at "the forks of the Ohio," that while they were doing so a French commander, Contrecoeur, arrived on the scene with 1200 Indians and soldiers and told Ward to leave.

Ward had no choice but to do so and followed this trail back to Virginia. Contrecoeur went on to built Ft. Duquesne.

Little more is known about activities at this fort.

Fort Field

The abandoned Roosevelt School along Rt. 51 at Large, site of the fort.

Lewis Run proceeds along the left of this picture and joins Peters Creek which runs along the trees in the background. The Dick Corp. office buildings are in the back of the photo, the school to the right.

Peters Creek near the point where it joins with Lewis Run. The easy availability of water was a necessity at these forts.

Cox's Fort

This fort was located in Union Township, Washington County, about one mile north of the village of Gastonville.

This site was the subject of an archaeological dig, authorized by the Pennsylvania Turnpike Commission, and performed by the firm of Skelly & Loy, Inc. of Monroeville. This was done in 1994 and various artifacts were unearthed. The study was not completed due to a change in plans by the Turnpike Commission.

To find this site get onto State Rt. 88 S and proceed to Finleyville. Just after entering this town turn left (east) on Washington Avenue. Follow this for .7 miles into Gastonville and to a stop sign. Here turn left (north) onto Stone Church Road and go 1.5 miles to the top of the hill and the State Historical Marker on the right side of the road. The James Chapel Methodist Church (established 1817) will be on your left.

The fort site is about three hundred yards to the east on land presently owned by Mr. & Mrs. Anthony Vaccari. You will observe a row of tress extending west to east and in the distance a north-south row of trees. The fort was at the junction of these rows of trees. A spring exists about two hundred feet northwest of the fort site.

Gabriel Cox came into this area around 1770 and received a Virginia Certificate in 1780 for 400 acres of land which he called "Coxburg." He was a Major under the authority of Virginia and participated in many Indian campaigns. At one time, in 1780, Virginia Land Commissioners actually met at this fort to adjudicate disputed land claims and issued Certificates. There is a deed to one Everhart Hupp for three hundred acres of land (on land which he apparently settled in 1769) and it concludes "Given under our hands at Cox's Fort the 18th day of February, 1780...." We are told that neighbors, who thought this was Pennsylvania land, were furious that a Virginia Commission should meet here.

It is known that militia were garrisoned here at some periods of time, and there is a pension application that states: "Dunlevy volunteered about the first of March, 1778, for one month's service. The rendezvous was at Cox's Station, on Peter's Creek."

Apparently there was a great deal of governmental and militia activity at this fort which may explain why there is no known record of any Indian attack. Sensible warriors would try to avoid places where there were concentrations of armed men.

Cox's Fort

This shows the north-south and east-west tree lines. The fort site was at their junction.

FORT COX OR COXES STATION

Built by Gabriel Cox about 700 yards Southeast of this site. Gabriel Cox came to this area in 1770 and took out a grant of 400 acres. The Virginia certificate was dated 1780 under the title of Coxburg. He also received another tract of 262 acres called Coxes addition. Here he built his log cabin near a spring of water on the present Waldo Brown farm. He also built a fort or blockhouse for protection from the Indians near the Brown and Denniston line fence, which later became a militia post. Gabriel Cox was a Major under the authority of Virginia from 1776 to 1781. He also was a participant in various expeditions that went out from this area against the Indians from 1778 to 1782. This was a stockade fort of considerable importance and was garrisoned by troops. It was used as headquarters for the land commissioners granting Virginia land certificates until sometime in 1780. This is shown by old certificates on record in the Recorder's office dated at Fort Cox.

PRESENT OWNER
ANTHONY VACCARI
PETERS CREEK HISTORICAL SOCIETY, INC.

The State Historical Marker along the road. The distance noted is wrong. It is closer to 400 yards.

Here, the fort site is to the right and the spring, about 200 feet from the fort, is at the opening in the trees at left-center of the pictures.

Bull Creek Blockhouse

The location of this site is unquestionably accurate and standing there, perhaps on the very foundation of the original, is a fine replica of a frontier blockhouse. Thanks for this extraordinary sight are owing to the Tarentum History and Landmarks Foundation. I believe that this is the <u>only</u> rebuilt blockhouse in southwestern Pennsylvania.

This blockhouse is located at the junction of the Allegheny River and Bull Creek. It sits in an attractive park which is a state-owned marina at the corner of First Street and Ross Street in Tarentum.

Incidentally this is the only fort in Allegheny County mentioned <u>in Frontier Forts of Western Pennsylvania</u>. That is a curiosity and represents very poor research since there were many frontier forts in this county.

Captain Robert Orr was a famous frontier leader and Indian fighter. In the summer of 1783 he raised a company of militia to serve for two months and "marched them to the mouth of Bull Creek, northwest of the Allegheny River, built a blockhouse there, and served out the necessary term." (Note the short period of time which these men agreed to serve - they simply couldn't leave their fields for a long time.)

It is very strange that he should have put a blockhouse at this location - along the west side of the Allegheny River - because that was clearly Indian country; there were no settlers on that side of the river (no legal ones, at least) and there was a Shawnee village up river only a few miles. Why here? What was Captain Orr thinking of? It wasn't a military outpost since there is no record of either militia units nor Army units manning it on a regular basis. Mr. Robert Lucas, a local historian, suggests that it was meant to be a refuge for the "spies" who were routinely sent across the Allegheny River to engage in long-range reconnaissance missions against the Indians as far west as middle Ohio and north to Lake Erie. On their return there would be occasions when they could not cross the river, due to floods, ice, or storms, and this blockhouse would offer a safe refuge. Another possibility is that it was used by Rangers routinely patrolling along the banks of the river on its west side looking for signs of war-parties who had crossed the river to raid the settlements. This would be a convenient place to rest for a day or two and also provide safety from any war-parties coming from the nearby Shawnee village or elsewhere.

We have no knowledge of any events occurring at this blockhouse nor the date it was torn down. Everything about it is shrouded in mystery. The earliest settlers who came here in the 1790's never mention it.

We can reasonably suspect that it was gone by 1791 because that is the year when the Indians raided through here and almost wiped out the Dary, Clark, and Cartwright families killing four men, two women, and six children. They had been "forted up" at Ross's cabin, only three miles up Bull Creek from this blockhouse. They seemed to have had some advance warning, and, surely, if this blockhouse had been in existence they would have come here. In addition, those who escaped the massacre ran all the way to this point along the Allegheny, then summoned help from across the river and were ferried to the other side. Obviously this would never have been done if this blockhouse had been in existence at that time.

So, the stories and tales are forever lost to us. The blockhouse stands there today as a silent symbol of that violent era.

Bull Creek Blockhouse

This view looks toward Bull Creek which can be seen to the right of the blockhouse. The Allegheny River is to the left.

This view shows the Tarentum bridge in the background going over the Allegheny River.

This shows the "overhang" of the second floor. Openings would have been made in it to enable settlers to fire down at Indians who were attempting to break in the door or set fire to the structure.

C. From the City of Washington West to the Ohio River

The Buffalo Creek area

Forts - East to West:

Wolff, Stricker, Taylor, Williamson, Lamb, Rice, Miller

Wolff's Fort

The site of this fort has been accurately located. It is in Buffalo Township, Washington county, four miles west of the city of Washington.

To get to this location proceed into the city of Washington and take US Rt. 40 W four miles to the site. It will be on the left side (south) of the road at a two-story red-brick house (built in the 1850's). The fort extended from the position of the house westward to the top of a hill. There is a state historical marker on the left (south) side of the road about 200 feet down the road from this house. It is at the wrong spot. For identification purposes, East Buffalo Church Road enters into US 40 about 100 feet west of the historical marker which would put it about 300 feet west of the house, and fort site.

The McDowell's were early settlers here and they acquired the portion of the Wolfe property that contained the fort. In 1850 the existing red-brick house was constructed by John McDowell.

Mrs. Joann McDowell Wetzel was kind enough to lead me around this property and point out the exact fort site, principally in the yard to the west of the house continuing to the nearby hillside overlooking US 40. She grew up in this house and only recently sold it. She is a very avid local historian and knows many of the old tales about the fort.

Jacob Wolff came here from Germany with his brother, John, and his wife, Elizabeth (or Barbara). They raised nine children on this property. Jacob's land consisted of 200 acres which he called "Wolff's Grove." It was warranted on April 23, 1793, and surveyed on September 3, 1793. Later he claimed an adjoining 244 acres. His brother, John, claimed land next to Jacob's property.

It is not known when they first arrived at this location, but they were among the very earliest settlers so that was probably in the early 1770's.

Jacob built a large fort with a stockade fence, and it was well-known and well-utilized as a place of refuge. There is a story that at one time a large body of Indians appeared before the fort with a white man in the uniform of a British Officer. He demanded the surrender of the fort, which demand was greeted with scorn by the inhabitants, and after exchanging several rifle shots, the Indians withdrew. That story has never been verified.

Other stories are well-documented.

William Darby wrote a letter in which he stated:

"We remained in Mr. Wolfe's house until February, 1782, while my father was preparing his cabin, into which we finally entered, but not to rest. In fifteen or twenty

157

days after our entrance to our log cabin, Martin Jolly came running breathless to tell us that a savage murder had been committed but ten miles distant. In two hours we were in Wolfe's Fort."

It didn't take these settlers long to get to a fort when they heard of Indian raids in the area.

Another sad tale which, again, illustrates the precipitous haste with which settlers left their homes, is that of Priscilla Peak. She was a young girl and was very sick and in bed when word came that Indians were close by and coming. Her family left her - one of them stopping to throw a blanket over her - and ran for their lives to Wolffe's Fort.

(I think this clearly shows the desperation of the frontierspeople and the awful choices they sometimes had to make. Probably there were other children in or around the house, and Mr. or Mrs. Peak were intent on saving as many as they could in the limited time they had. There was no hope of carrying Priscilla when they may have had a baby to carry and toddlers they had to help scurry along. These terrible choices often appear in the literature. See Rice's Fort where children were locked out of the blockhouse!)

At any rate, Priscilla dragged herself out of bed, staggered out into the yard, and collapsed against the fence surrounding a pig-pen. Here an Indian warrior found her, very callously scalped her without killing her, and threw her aside. After they left, Priscilla, with bleeding scalp and still terribly sick, crawled on her hands and knees to Wolff's Fort. She recovered but wore a black cap over the ugly wound for the rest of her life.

Then there is the tale of the beautiful Lydia Boggs (the Belle of the Frontier), and her friend Christianna Clemmens who lived near Taylor's Fort, but were cut off from it by some Indians in October, 1784. They ran for Wolff's Fort as fast as they ever ran in their lives and made it, breathless, clothes torn and badly scratched, but safe.

A famous romance blossomed here between Hugh Brackenridge, a prominent young lawyer, and Servenia Wolff, Jacob's daughter. They finally married and Hugh went on to become a Pennsylvania Supreme Court Justice. It is interesting that after their marriage Servenia went to Philadelphia to pursue her higher education and then returned here.

Wolff's Fort

This sign, along Rt. 40, is about two hundred feet west of where it ought to be.

This house, built in 1850, stands at the fort site. The fort, and stockade fence, extended westwardly into the picture. Mrs. Joann McDowell Wetzel, who grew up here and owned this house, stands at or near the easterly end of the fort.

This view, from the westerly end of the fort site, overlooks Rt. 40 and the countryside. Taylor's Fort would have been about 3 miles beyond the hills from this site.

Stricker's Blockhouse

This site has been accurately located. It is one mile south of Wolfe's Fort.

From the city of Washington, proceed 4 miles on US 40 west to the site of Wolfe's Fort. There is a State Marker on the left side of the road. One hundred yards beyond this marker and on the left is East Buffalo Church Road. Turn left on to this road and proceed .4 mile. Doman Lane is a dirt and gravel lane on the left. Proceed down Doman Lane to the end (private property). The home of Mr. Lonnie Doman is at that point. A few feet beyond, in the side yard, is the site of Stricker's Blockhouse.

Mr. Doman is a Senior Citizen and former public official who is knowledgeable concerning the history of the area. He has lived on this property since 1934. He recalls seeing the foundation ruins. His uncle, Henry Mounts, was born in the 1870's and lived in this area until his death in the 1950's. He explained to Mr. Doman that in his youth a substantial portion of the old blockhouse was still in existence.

Mr. Earle Forrest took a photograph of the foundation ruins in the early 1920's and that is shown here.

The blockhouse stood on a point of land about 20 feet above a ravine which runs to the west on one side and a broad valley to the east which extends north and south. A road once ran through that valley to Rt. 40 near Wolfe's Fort.

In the ravine, about 100 feet to the west is the original spring, still in use today. Mr. Doman built the present structure which covers it.

Lawrence Stricker was one of the first white men in this area, Buffalo Township, Washington County. His land contained 369 1/4 acres, was surveyed on April 28, 1786, and he was granted a Virginia Certificate. He called it "Prulie" and what that means we will never know.

Stricker built two blockhouses on his property. Why this was done and whether they existed contemporaneously or were successive structures we do not know. The other one lies to the west about five hundred yards on the far side of East Buffalo Church Road.

This was the larger structure and has been described as being 40 feet square on the first floor, the second floor slightly larger.

There is a story that a tiny room was built off the cellar as an extension in the foundation. This was constructed as a hiding place should the blockhouse be overrun by Indians. It could be utilized by moving some stones of the "regular foundation," crawling into the room, and then shoving those stones back into position.

This was a substantial blockhouse and only one mile away was the large Wolfe's Fort. The interesting question springs to mind why these structures were needed so close together? Either the families nearby were so large that two forts were required to house them, or possibly, Indian raids were so frequent that the settlers believed they wouldn't have time to walk the extra mile. Many war-parties came from the south and perhaps those families south of Stricker's felt that they could get as far as his place but never to Wolfe's Fort, and thus this blockhouse was constructed.

There are no records of raids at this site, although there are stories of raids at Wolfe's Fort. (See) However, because of the close proximity, raiding parties at one place necessarily required "forting up" at the other.

There is a traditional story of one young girl, a McDowell, racing for her life toward Stricker's with some Indians behind her when, suddenly, a war-party appeared ahead of her cutting her off from the blockhouse. She veered into a rocky area and found a crevice between two rocks into which she squeezed and hid until dark. That night she crept away and made it to Stricker's and safety.

The foundation stone with the year inscribed "1795" is across the ravine from the blockhouse site, to the north, and what building it supported is not known.

Stricker's Blockhouse

This building stood on the point of land between the two valleys.

It was in the side yard of the Doman property and in front of the barn.

The springhouse was about 150 feet away and this structure is at that site.

Taylor's Fort

This site has been accurately located.

From Pittsburgh you may take Interstate 70 south to Exit 3, turn right on to State Route 221 heading northwest, and into Taylorstown which is a small village. In the center of town turn right, still on Rt. 221, now called Buffalo Creek Road, and proceed .4 mile. At this point there is an old iron bridge on the right going over Buffalo Creek. On the left is a fifteen foot bluff. Taylor's Fort stood on the level ground at the top of this embankment.

This fort is mentioned by the Rev. Doddridge but practically nothing is known about activities at the fort. Certainly the Buffalo Creek area was a hot-bed of Indian raids but no specifics are available as to occurrences here.

There is a reference in the book Frontier Retreat On The Upper Ohio (p.110) of an order dated November 8, 1779, directing all Militia Captains in the area to meet on Monday, December 27, 1779, at the residence of Robert Taylor, himself a Captain. We may reasonably assume that this residence was at Taylor's Fort. The various Captains were to prepare and present a roster of all the effective men in their respective companies.

This fort is also mentioned by Earle Forrest in his History of Washington County and he states "Built at a date unknown..."

Taylor's Fort

The fort was located on this plateau overlooking Buffalo Creek to the right.

This view shows the old iron bridge that goes over the creek.

The road makes a sharp left curve here going around the fort site. The road to the right is an intersecting road going over the bridge.

Williamson's Station

This site has been accurately located thanks to the efforts of Mr. Ronald W. Eisert, formerly a Field Associate of the Carnegie Museum of National History, and an archaeologist.

It is difficult, but fun, to get to this site.

From Pittsburgh proceed on Interstate 70 west to Exit 3. Turn right on to State Rt. 221, heading northwestwardly to Taylorstown. In the middle of that village turn right onto Buffalo Creek Road (still Rt. 221) and proceed 3.2 miles to a red covered bridge on the left. (You will have passed the site of Taylor's Fort which is .4 miles from the middle of Taylorstown).

Turn left and go through the red covered bridge and proceed .2 miles to Camp Buffalo Road. Turn right on to this road and you will immediately cross Nobles Bridge over Buffalo Creek. Proceed .7 miles from the bridge to the second "Jeep Tail" on the right. Park at this spot. This lane, or "Jeep Trail," goes up hill and you must proceed on foot. At about 250 yards the lane curves to the right. At this curve turn off to the left and walk through the underbrush about 100 to 125 feet. There you will find, in a ravine, the springhouse ruins. The foundation ruins of the old farmhouse are located about 100 feet away, further up the lane, but still about 100 to 125 feet away from it.

The lane proceeds in a rough northeast, southwest direction and these ruins would be on the northwest side of the lane, about 100 feet apart.

Incidentally the farmhouse was destroyed by a tornado which came through here in 1944.

Earle Forrest found and photographed the springhouse in 1922 and that photograph is shown.

This station was established by Col. David Williamson at a date unknown, but probably around 1776. It was a large fort consisting of three buildings, each about 20 x 20 feet and at least one of them was built in the blockhouse style. One of the buildings was constructed over the spring. A stockade fence is believed to have surrounded the area and probably the exterior wall of the three buildings was the stockade wall in that area where they stood. This, of course, was the traditional manner of construction.

Co. Williamson was a very famous person of the time, noted for his bravery and Indian fighting skills, and he led the (much condemned) expedition against the Moravian Indians at Gnadenhutten, Ohio. He was also the second-in-command of the ill-fated Crawford Expedition (June, 1782), and when the rout occurred he is credited with holding together the remains of that panic-stricken expedition and getting the men back to Pittsburgh.

In later years Col. Williamson was three times elected by his fellow citizens to be Justice of the Peace. Like all of us he had detractors - the County Prothonotary wrote a nasty letter recommending that he not be permitted to serve saying "...he is a foolish (gawky), impertinent, and insolent boy, totally void of all the necessary qualifications for so important a trust."

Nonetheless, Williamson got the job. He died a pauper, by the way.

Nothing is known about daily activities or Indian raids at this location, nor the number of families who "forted" here.

Suffice it to say that the raids came often as they did for all of the Buffalo Creek area and that the fort was well used.

Ruins of the old Springhouse built at Colonel David Williamson's Fort on Buffalo Creek, Donegal Township. This springhouse was built at the same time as the fort, shortly after 1780. The spring furnished water for the fort. Tradition tells us that the great oak seen here was standing then. Photo taken in 1922.

This picture is from Earle Forrest's *History of Washington County.*

These are the springhouse ruins today. This is a "head-on" view whereas Forrest took his photo at an angle to the left of the ruins.

This view is from the hillside above the springhouse ruins, perhaps thirty feet away. The position is slightly beyond the oak tree, toward the house, in the Forrest picture. Here Mr. Gaetano stands at the closest side of the farmhouse foundation.

Lamb's Fort

The site of this fort has been located in Independence Township, Washington County. It was situated on State Rt. 331 W two hundred yards west of the intersection of State Rts. 331 W and 231 N.

This fort was erected by Frederick Lamb in 1774 and was one of several in the Dutch Fork region of Buffalo Creek. Rice's Fort was about four miles south, Miller's Blockhouse just beyond that, and Williamson's Station is about two miles to the east.

This fort was a log structure about twenty feet square and one and one-half stories high. The upper story was a single room. There were two windows on the north side, one in each story, a window on the east side of the first floor, and the entrance was on the west side of the north corner. On the south side was a fireplace and large chimney.

The fort stood along side of Rt. 331, Brush Run Road, and the foundation, some of the logs, and the chimney were still standing in 1932. At that time the state widened and hard-surfaced Rt. 331 and in so doing the chimney was removed and the south side of the building fell into disrepair. By 1937 the last vestiges of the fort were gone.

Mr. Roy Keenan lives in the house about one-half mile west of the fort site. He and his sister, Mabel Kennell, both Senior Citizens, vividly recall seeing the foundation ruins and have researched the history of the place.

About one mile west of the Keenan house and along the road can be seen the existing ruins of the Fergus Smith cabin built in 1813. These ruins are rapidly deteriorating.

When Rice's Fort was attacked by Indians on September 13, 1782, Abraham Rice rode to Lambs's Fort for help and to have his wounds attended to. Here he gathered a small party of men and sped to the relief of his own fort. For further details see the information on Rice's Fort.

Little more is known about events at this fort. Certainly the Dutch Fork region was continuously harassed by Indians for twenty years or more but, unfortunately, we have no records nor details of the people and the things that happened at this site.

Lamb's Fort

These photos show the site as seen from Rt. 331. The first is looking west; the second, northwest; and the third looking north. The foundation ruins were still in existence in the 1930's, close to the road, but were destroyed by the road construction.

Rice's Fort

This fort was one of the most well known, and oft-used, defensive positions on this part of the western frontier. It was located along the Dutch Fork of Buffalo Creek, and the entire Buffalo Creek area was ablaze with Indian fighting for decades.

It is also the only fort for which we have an accurate sketch made while it was still in existence. This drawing was made in 1811 and shows three blockhouses, interconnected. There was no stockade fence. A spring, still existing, is about 200 feet to the west of the fort.

The site has been accurately located and it is amusing to note that the State has a historical marker four miles away but none at the scene.

The fort site is in Donegal Township, Washington County, just north of Dutch Fork Lake. Proceed down I-70 W to Exit 2, Claysville. Turn right for 100 feet then a left onto US Rt. 40 W. Follow this road for 2.7 miles to Lake Road which will be on your right (north). Incidentally, at this junction, on the left side of US 40 is the State historical marker above referred to. Turn right (north) on Lake Road and go 3.2 miles. For identification purposes, at 3.1 miles you will see a road on the right entering Lake Road and a small bridge going over Dutch Fork. The site is .1 miles further north on Lake Road. Look for a two-story red-brick house and detached red garage on your left (west), the home of the Craig Moore family, 683 Lake Road. Behind their house is a thirty foot embankment with a large, level field at its top. The fort stood in that field close to the hillside. The fort property is owned by Mr. James Moore, brother of Craig Moore.

To give perspective to the numbers of these forts, two miles south is Miller's Blockhouse, three miles north is Lamb's Fort, three miles east is Williamson's Station, and a little east of that is Taylor's Fort, then Wolfe's Fort - all in the Buffalo Creek area.

I could regale you for pages with tales of happenings at Rice's Fort. Naturally the stories would necessarily involve all of the other forts mentioned above. When word was carried that "Indians are coming" all families within a radius of ten miles stopped what they were doing and raced for "their" fort. No one could be sure what direction a war-party might decide to go and no one could take chances.

As one example of the devastation a single war-party caused in the vicinity of this fort, on September 9, 1781, Wyandot warriors killed William Huston in his cornfield. Two hours later they killed Jesse Cochran, and later in the day caught Benjamin Roger in his field and killed him. The next day, September 10, they chased William Ayres almost to within sight of this fort and killed him. Later that day they ambushed and killed Captain Sam Teeter and an unknown man riding with him near the fort. These were just two routine days on the frontier.

The most famous event occurring at this fort is the raid of September 14-15 of 1782 by about 70 warriors. The neighbors had about thirty minutes warning. Everyone rushed to the fort, but several children and teenagers were out in the orchards and were literally locked out of the fort!

The Indians struck at breakfast time and quickly killed one man and a child. They came from the orchard area - the hillside to the west, behind the fort. Several teenagers found a ladder and scrambled up to a window to get in. One girl was hit and also a boy who had just reached the top of the ladder when he was struck in the leg by a bullet and had his femur fractured.

Another child was hit just outside the wall and the women and boys tore up the floor boards, desperately dug a hole under the wall of the building, and dragged the child inside. It was dead.

There were only six men to defend the fort and two were assigned to each blockhouse. (Several other men had just gone to Hagerstown, Maryland, to trade furs for much needed salt, ammunition, and iron.)

The fact that six men could hold off seventy Indians is testimony to the safety of these blockhouses once the settlers got inside and "buttoned-up," combined with the deadly accuracy of those Pennsylvania Rifles in the hands of skilled frontiersmen. Only one man, inside, was killed in the fight.

Those blockhouses were extremely difficult to attack successfully.

The Indians then drifted down to the creek area and heavy firing went on for four hours. The women in the fort made ammunition and cut linen patches while the men fired.

Abraham Rice was away at the time but heard the firing and rode in great haste for the fort. He came over the hill to the east, on the far side of the creek, and in an almost suicidal attempt tried to ride through the Indians. He was shot in the arm and thigh as his horse stumbled through the water, and he was forced to turn and ride away. He took off for Lamb's Fort three miles away and arrived there faint from loss of blood. He was treated, some neighbors were gathered together, and that night he insisted on going with them to the relief of the fort. They arrived in the dead of night and could see by the flashes of the Indian rifles that the fighting was still going on and where the warrior line was located. There were just too many of those bright yellow rifle flashes for ten of the men, and they elected to go back to Lamb's Fort. Rice and two men crawled forward but they were eventually discovered, the

Indians raised a cry, and these men had to hastily crawl and dodge back to their horses and race back to Lamb's Fort.

About 10 o'clock that night the Indians set fire to the barn, located in the valley below the fort and about 60 yards away. Mercifully a gentle wind blew the flames and sparks to the southeast, away from the fort, and no harm was caused by this blaze except that the bright light allowed for a flare-up in the firing.

Sometime in the wee hours of the morning the Indians slipped away.

Sixty men gathered the next day at the fort and started out to trail the Indians. After about two miles they found that the warriors had split up into small parties and scattered. The settlers gave up the pursuit.

One of those small war-parities, on their way home, killed four more settlers.

Rice's Fort

The fort stood on this plateau about twenty feet above the Miller House on the right. The road runs in front of the house and the creek is along the trees in the distance. Abraham Rice came over the hill in the background and tried to cross the creek to go to the defense of the fort.

The hillside is quite steep separating the upper plateau from the land below. The original Indian attack was from the orchard to the rear of the photo.

The Indians came down to the creek and did most of their fighting from here. The white house is just about at the location of the barn which was set afire. The fort would be to the right on top of the embankment.

Rice's Fort

This view is from the fort site looking west toward where the orchard was located. Initially, the Indians came from this direction.

This looks east toward the road and the creek beyond. The barn would have been to the right of this picture.

The Indians were scattered along this creek and it was near this point that Abraham Rice tried to cross and was shot and wounded.

MAP BASED ON ISAAC LEFFLER'S
Pen Sketch of Rice's Fort

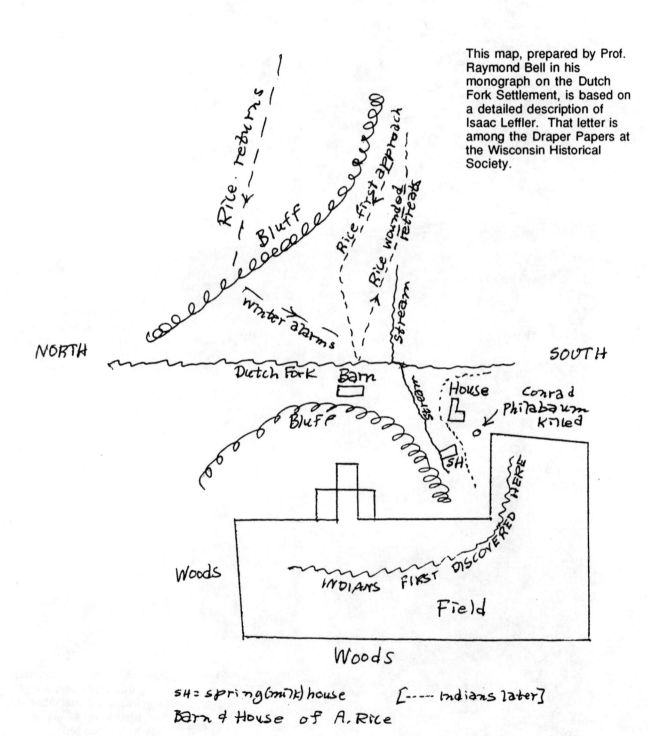

This map, prepared by Prof. Raymond Bell in his monograph on the Dutch Fork Settlement, is based on a detailed description of Isaac Leffler. That letter is among the Draper Papers at the Wisconsin Historical Society.

Rice returns

Bluff

Rice first approach

Rice wounded retreats

winter alarms

stream

NORTH

SOUTH

Dutch Fork

Barn

House

Conrad Philabaum killed

Bluff

SH

INDIANS FIRST DISCOVERED HERE

Woods

Field

Woods

SH = spring (milk) house   [----- Indians later]

Barn & House of A. Rice

This is a drawing of Rice's Fort, made in 1811. The original is among the Draper Papers at the Wisconsin Historical Society in Madison, Wisconsin. It is the only drawing we have of a settlers fort made while it was still in existence.

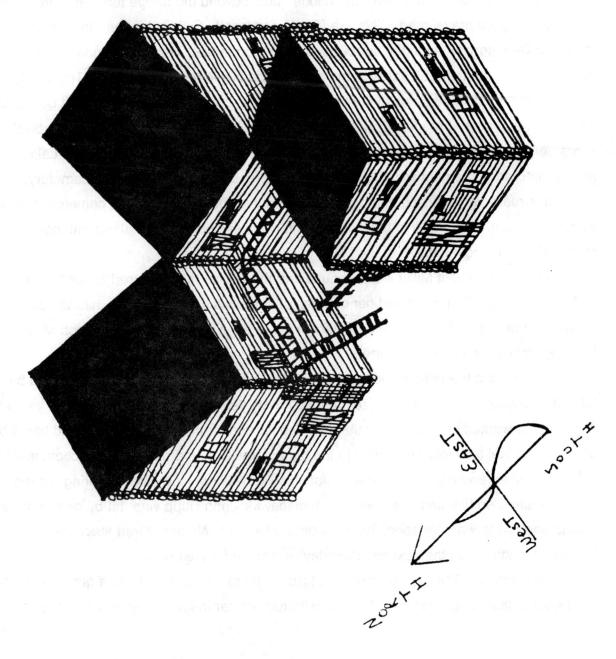

Miller's Blockhouse

This site has been accurately located. It is in Donegal Township, Washington County, just 1 1/2 miles north of US Rt. 40.

The easiest way to get to this location is to get on to Interstate 70 west and exit at Interchange 2, Claysville. Turn right for 100 feet and immediately turn left onto US Rt. 40 W. Proceed for 2.7 miles to Lake Road which enters from the right (north). Turn right (north) on Lake Road and go on for .1 miles. At this point you are at the southerly edge of Dutch Fork Lake. Turn right (east) and go over the bridge. Just beyond the bridge turn left (north) and proceed along the gravel road. This is a (State) park road. Follow this road for 1.3 miles to the Miller Cemetery on the right, surrounded by an iron fence. The road bends left at this point. Proceed another 150 yards to the parking and picnic area at the lake. The blockhouse site is off-shore about 50 yards to the right of the road - it would be the south-east corner of the lake at that spot. For identification purposes the blockhouse was about two hundred yards from the cemetery. When the State took over the land to create Dutch Fork Lake it entered into an agreement with the Miller heirs to preserve and maintain the cemetery.

It is really very startling and poignant to find this small, well-tended, cemetery here in a wild, lonely spot, off by itself in the woods. Ann Hupp lies buried here along with her husband, John, and members of the Miller family.

The stories about Miller's Blockhouse and the events that occurred around it are legion. The tale of Ann Hupp and her defense of it on March 31, 1782, has already been told. It was a rendezvous for scouts and rangers in the area. Young Capt. John Jacob Miller and his rangers used it as a headquarters.

There are a few details about the attack of Easter Morning, 1782, that remain to be told. Jacob Miller was a Senior citizen that day, sixty years old. John Hupp was 35 years old. Ann had not wanted them to go out that morning looking for that lost colt. She had had a bad dream. The trail they followed led off to the right of the lake, in a northeast direction, and they were ambushed about 300 yards away. Jacob Miller was not hit by the first firing but the Indians rushed on him and killed him with tomahawks; John Hupp was hit by one or more bullets and ran forward for about 70 yards before he died. No one dared leave the blockhouse until Noon the next day (Monday) to search for their bodies.

Ann was undoubtedly heartbroken at the death of her husband. She gathered up her children, left this area, and went off to live with her brother-in-law, Philip Hupp, some considerable distance away. She stayed with him for four years then came back here and married John May.

Think for a moment about these pioneer women: Ann was 25 years old when all this happened. She had lost her mother, two brothers, and a husband to Indians and had to fight for her own life on this occasion. If she and her children were filled with hatred for Indians, they had a right to those feelings. The amazing thing about these women is that most of them stayed and kept struggling. They lived on. Incredible. How did they do it?

I could go on endlessly with stories. Capt. John, Jacob Miller's son, was captured by Indians near here. In the dead of night he gnawed through the leather thongs that bound his hands and got away. Tough kid, he was only 19 years old.

The Hawkin's cabin was built on a bluff overlooking a stream a few miles from here. The Indians attacked it one day. Mrs. Hawkins grabbed her baby, went over the bluff and into the stream. She waded through it for some distance then turned into a little run that came down to the stream. She followed it, then climbed up the bank and ran until she found a fallen tree and hid amongst the foliage. The Indians followed her up the stream but failed to turn off at the run. After going on for some time, they left the stream, spread out, and doubled back toward the cabin looking for her. They passed by the fallen tree within a few feet of where she lay. She nearly killed the baby jamming her apron in its mouth to keep it from crying. She lay there all night in a pouring rain. The next day Rangers, out scouting, found her and took her to this blockhouse.

It was a wonderful life - a gay old time. A "simpler, slower" way of life, we like to say today.

Who are we kidding?

Miller's Blockhouse

This shows the southeast corner of Dutch Fork Lake and the approximate position of the blockhouse, about 100 feet into the lake.

This photo taken by Earle Forrest about 1917. It appears in his "History of Washington County."

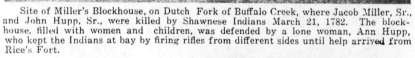

Site of Miller's Blockhouse, on Dutch Fork of Buffalo Creek, where Jacob Miller, Sr., and John Hupp, Sr., were killed by Shawnese Indians March 21, 1782. The blockhouse, filled with women and children, was defended by a lone woman, Ann Hupp, who kept the Indians at bay by firing rifles from different sides until help arrived from Rice's Fort.

This picture looks east along the shore of the lake. The cemetery is to the upper right about 150 yards away.

Miller's Blockhouse

The Miller Cemetery off in the woods by itself, a very lonely, poignant spot. It was about 200 yards from the blockhouse.

The grave of Ann Hupp within the cemetery. Jacob Miller and John Hupp are also buried here.

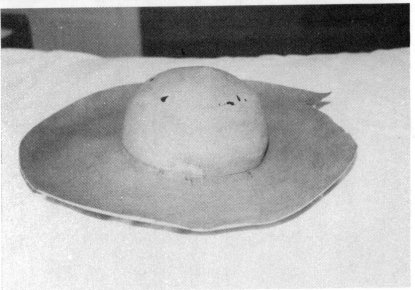

The hat worn by Jacob Miller at the time of his death is at the Washington County Historical Society. The holes are the result of "wear and tear." He was killed with tomahawk blows.

D. <u>Western Washington County in the Vicinity</u> of the City of Avella

The Cross Creek Area

Forts:

Reynolds, Wells, Teeter, Doddridge

Reynold's Blockhouse

The location of this blockhouse has been precisely determined. It is in Cross Creek Township, Washington County.

From Pittsburgh take Interstate 79 S to the Bridgeville exit. Turn right on to State Rt. 50 W. Proceed about fifteen miles to State Rt. 18 N. Turn right and go on to Atlasburg. Turn left on to Cross Creek Road and proceed 2 miles to the village of Cross Creek. Turn left on to Parker Road (at the Cross Creek Presbyterian Church) and proceed .1 miles to a "Y." Stay to the right on Parker Road and go 1.2 miles to the lane leading back to the farm of Sylvester Casciola, whose address is 559 Parker Road. The blockhouse stood at the location of the present black-roofed barn and brown silo. The springhouse is still in its original location and contains some of the original foundation stones. It is about seventy-five feet from the blockhouse site. A stockade fence undoubtedly encircled the blockhouse and spring.

William Reynolds came to this area in 1775 and claimed 399 acres on a Virginia Certificate. It was surveyed on December 4, 1785, and was called "Reynoldsville."

The blockhouse was built in 1775 and provided protection to Mr. Reynolds, his wife and child, and also the families of James Jackson, James Colwell, Ephraim Hart, and the widow Mary Patterson.

Sadly, it wasn't enough to protect Mrs. Reynolds and her baby. In the summer of 1779 , while Mr. Reynolds was gone, a raiding party of Indians came by and captured Mrs. Reynolds and her baby. Sometime later Reynolds came home and discovered his loss. He quickly rounded up the Rev. Thomas Marquis (note the active role of the clergy of the time), his brother John Marquis, and Robert McCreedy and the four men picked up the Indian trail and started after them. They eventually caught up with the war-party but, apparently, failed to approach the Indians with caution; it is possible that they inadvertently stumbled onto the Indians. In either event, the warriors did their usual thing when surprised - they killed Mrs. Reynolds and the baby, then scattered and disappeared.

The men brought back the two bodies, and it is believed, they are buried in the Cross Creek Cemetery.

William Reynolds was simply heartbroken by these events and refused to return to his home. Shortly thereafter he sold the farm to Joseph Patterson. A few years later he moved to Ohio where he lived the remainder of his life.

We can take a moment to wonder about the Rev. Marquis. While on the trail of those Indians he was out to kill, if it came to fighting, and he was probably as proficient with a rifle as most men of his time. I wonder what he had to say to William Reynolds? To his congregation at his next sermon? How did he square the violent reality of the times with the Gospel messages of love, forgiveness, and charity? Especially when he knew there could be another Indian raid tomorrow or next week or next month - and more dead parishioners. The clergymen of the time were, for the most part, very serious, devout persons who had studied for the ministry and understood their religion and theology. This must have been a very troubling time for them. They were dealing with a suffering, enraged, and therefore irrational congregation, and it would be useless, probably counter-productive, to preach about love and understanding toward Indians. No, that couldn't be done. I, for one, wonder what the Rev. Marquis did say at his next sermon. What do you think?

Reynold's Blockhouse

The blockhouse was located at the site of the barn shown in the center of this picture.

The exact position was at this silo and included a few feet of the barn. This photo is taken from a position near to the springhouse.

This shows the springhouse about 100 feet from the blockhouse site. Some of the foundation stones are believed to be original.

Well's Fort

This fort was very well known on the frontier and it was located at the junction of the north and south forks of Cross Creek in Cross Creek Township, Washington County. The reason for its notoriety is the fact that Alexander Wells had a grist mill there which provided flour for a large number of settlers in the vicinity, and it was the only such mill in the area.

There is some dispute as to the exact location: most knowledgeable persons place it on the creek; a few claim that it was at a plateau on a nearby hill about 300 yards north of the stream. The preponderance of the evidence, and a certain amount of logic, places it on the stream where it could easily protect the grist mill.

The site is right in the middle of the town of Avella where State Rt. 50, coming from the east, stops at a "T" intersection. The fort was along the creek at the white building at the center of the "T". Frontier Forts of Western Pennsylvania (P. 421) states that:

> "Besides being a refuge for the families of the settlement it was also a defense for the mill which stood a few rods west of it...." (This clearly places it on the creek.)

It goes on to comment that this was one of the earliest mills built in this part of the country.

Alexander Wells came into this country in 1773, but when he built the fort and mill is unknown. He called his land "Mayfield."

It is interesting to note that a general store was opened here as early as 1795. Crumrine, in his "History of Washington County," reports an advertisement that was posted on October 25, 1795:

> "John Kerr & Co. have opened and are now selling at Alexander Well's mill, on Cross Creek, a neat assortment of merchandise suitable for the season, for cash or country produce."

It's sort of odd to think of a country store operating in this wild place at that time. Another touch of civilization intrudes on the frontier!

The grist mill was very important to the people. General George Rogers Clark, planning an attack on Indians, was worried about supplies for his soldiers, and noted in a letter dated July 2, 1781 "...there is a considerable quantity of flour at Well's...Mill to be lodged at Coxe's Fort on the Ohio River."

A large group of settlers petitioned General Irvine to send some militia to protect this mill saying (May 2, 1782):

> "We, the inhabitants, who live near Mr. Alex. Wells' mill, being very unhandy to any other mill, and daily open and exposed to the rage of a savage and merciless

enemy...cannot continue to make a stand without some assistance. And it is clear that if this mill is evacuated many of the adjacent forts, at least seven or eight, that now hope to make a stand, must give up; as their whole dependence is on said mill for bread as well as every expedition from these parts. And scouting parties that turn out on alarms are supplied from here."

Their letter did some good - General Irvine did station militia soldiers at this fort.

That these people did face a "merciless and savage enemy" is illustrated by the story of Mrs. Glass who lived nearby. On March 27, 1789, two Indians captured her, her two small sons, an African-American slave woman, and her son. They ransacked the cabin then started off with the prisoners. After a short distance they murdered the child of the slave woman.

Mr. Glass came home sometime later, saw the state of affairs, and ran to Well's Fort for help. A party of ten men was quickly gathered and they picked up the trail at the Glass cabin. It was providential that Mrs. Glass wore shoes with high heels for they left a distinct impression in the grass and dirt that made the trail easy to follow. The Indians crossed the Ohio River with their prisoners, went on for a distance, and then camped for the night. Perhaps the white men would never have found the place of crossing except that the four year old Glass boy had carried with him a piece of white paper and this was dropped at the place the party landed on the west side of the river. The frontiersmen saw it and picked up the trail again. They found the camp, charged it quickly, wounded and drove off the Indians, and effected a rescue of the women and children.

That was just another incident on the frontier.

Well's Fort

This is the very center of Avella. The building on the left marks the fort site.

This view looks east from behind the buildings shown above. Some people claim the fort was on the hillside at top-left of this picture. However, the preponderance of evidence places it here, to protect the mill.

This shows the junction of the two forks of Cross Creek. The grist mill would have been to the south, to the bottom of this picture, but relatively close by.

Teeter's Fort

The location of this fort is beyond doubt - it is at the site of the beautiful home known as Manchester House and which is on the National Registry of Historic Places. Two of the original foundation stones may been in the front yard of this building and the spring is just a few feet to the east of the house.

This home is presently owned by the Eugene Painter family.

To get to this location proceed from Avella in Washington County on State Rt. 50 W for one mile to a "Y" in the road. Bear left at this point onto Route 231 S for one more mile to the top of the hill. A private lane joins the highway here, on the left (east) side of the road, and leads to the house, located in the valley and which can be seen from the highway.

Captain Samuel Teeter settled in this area in 1773 along with The Wells and Doddridge families. His wife was Mary Doddridge and he was the uncle of the Rev. Joseph Doddridge. He owned 1000 acres which he called "Plantation Plenty." He was born in 1737 and served in the Braddock Expedition of 1755 when he would have been 18 years old, and in the successful Forbes Campaign of 1758 at the age 21. Most likely he was a part of the Virginia Rangers under George Washington.

We know that this fort occupied one-eighth of an acre and had a stockade fence around it and the nearby spring. We also know that it fell into a state of disrepair for some reason and that thereafter the Teeter family "forted up" at Doddridge's Fort, about 3/4 mile away to the southwest. This is a curiosity. One possible explanation is that the Indian raids were so frequent and violent that Captain Teeter thought his fort was too small for safety and he then got together with the Doddridges and agreed to build a large, substantial fort on the Doddridge property. We know this was done.

A son of his, also Samuel, was with an unknown friend when they were ambushed and killed near Rice's Fort, about seven miles away.

Captain Teeter sold his land to Isaac Manchester in 1797, emigrated to Ohio, and died at Marysville, Ohio on October 8, 1823.

Isaac Manchester began work on this mansion, a fifteen room dwelling, in 1800, and it took him fifteen years to compete it. Quite obviously it is an outstanding example of the architecture of the early 1800's.

Little more is known about events occurring at this fort.

We do know that a major Indian attack was once expected at Doddridge's Fort, that Captain Teeter moved his family into that fort for protection, and that he was voted to be in command of the defense there. For more details refer to Doddridge's Fort.

Teeter's Fort

This beautiful home is Manchester House built between 1800 and 1815. The fort stood in the front yard and, in the bottom picture, Mr. Albert Miller points to one of two foundation stones that are still present. The spring was by the large tree that appears in the background of the middle picture.

Doddridge's Fort

This fort is certainly one of the best known on the frontier by virtue of the writing of the Rev. Joseph Doddridge, "The Settlement and Indian Wars of the Western Parts of Virginia and Pennsylvania, 1763-1783." He grew up here and writes about frontier days in fascinating detail. Much of what we know about those days is due to his book.

The location of this fort is accurate and beyond doubt. It is in Independence Township, Washington County, along State Rt. 884, about three miles west of the village of West Middletown. There is a State Historical Marker standing at the junction of Rt. 884 and Sugar Run Road.

To reach this site proceed to the town of Avella and there follow State Rt. 50 W about five miles to Independence. Then turn left (east) on State Rt. 884 for two miles to the historical marker at the site. The fort stood on the plateau on the north side of the road and a white house is at that location at the present time.

An uncle of Joseph Doddridge, Samuel Teeter, had his fort about 3/4 of a mile to the north. If you follow Sugar Run Road to its end, Teeter's Fort was in the valley directly across the road. This fort fell into disrepair and thereafter the Teeter family "forted' at Doddridge's.

At Doddridge's, a stockade fence enclosed about one-half an acre and for some strange reason the nearby spring was not included. We know this because when the fort was about to be attacked the women were directed to take every container they could find, fill it with water at the spring, and carry it into the fort.

John Doddridge brought his family here, from Bedford, in 1773. He took up 437 acres of land under a Virginia Certificate that was surveyed on April 6, 1786, and called by him "Extravagance." That's another odd name.

The fort served twelve surrounding families and the central blockhouse was still standing in 1913.

The Rev. Doddridge tells us about the preparations at the fort for a threatened Indian attack. They first elected Samuel Teeter to be their commander. His orders to the women are given earlier in this book. He told the men to cut their bullets smaller than usual and to use rifle patches thinner than normal and they were to be well-oiled. His greatest fear was a jammed rifle in a critical moment of the fight. "Have the locks well oiled, and your flints sharp, so as not to miss fire." He seriously expected that the Indians might get inside the stockade walls because he directed everyone to bring into their little shacks tomahawks, axes, mattocks, and hoes for a fight to the finish. Every man was assigned a port hole in the blockhouse or around the stockade. Everyone - man, woman, and child was warned to expect no mercy from the Indians if they should be defeated. The attack was expected to occur a little after dawn.

This was deadly serious business and it is very hard for us to imagine the worry and concern involved in these preparations. None of us has ever been threatened like this in our entire lives. We get upset if we simply read about a "drive-by shooting" that occurred twenty miles away or an explosion that killed people 2,000 miles away. What must it have been like to actually witness some Indians killing your relatives in a field just beyond your house and know that when they finished they were coming after you? Suddenly the whole affair would take on a different aspect; it would no longer be an academic matter, it would be real and deadly.

Today we love to sit back and pontificate in lofty terms of love, understanding, sympathy, and tolerance. Oh yeah! Back then, amidst the real blood and gore of your mother or son, you would have hated, cursed, and fought.

A lot of that went on at Doddridge's Fort and the surrounding countryside. We will never understand what it was like.

Doddridge's Fort

The site of Doddridge's Fort.

State Historical Marker along the road.

THE EARLY DODDRIDGE HOME IN 1911.

Built by John Doddridge at a date unknown. Probably the first dwelling erected in Independence township, Washington county, Pa.

This photo is taken from the Heritage Books reprint of Rev. Doddridge's classic frontier book. (See bibliography.) This house was probably near to, but not a part of, the fort complex.

194

Site of Doddridge's Blockhouse, three miles west of West Middletown. Built by John Doddridge in 1772. Torn down in 1913. This shows the foundation stones and a few of the logs.

Doddridge's Fort

Top: Photo taken by Earle Forrest about 1917 and in his "History of Washington County."

Middle: Photo taken in 1994 from about the same location.

Bottom: Another photo taken by Earle Forrest showing the springhouse.

Bottom Right: A picture of the springhouse today.

Springhouse near Doddridge's Blockhouse, built about 75 years ago from logs of the original stockade around the blockhouse.

E. Southern Washington County; Greene County

Blockhouse Run, Ten Mile Creek, Wheeling Creek, and Whitely Creek areas

Forts:

Roney, Campbell, Lindley, Ryerson, Garard

Roney's Blockhouse

This site had been accurately located. Our guide was Mr. John Roney who is a direct descendent of the founding family and who lives on a portion of the ancestral lands. He is well acquainted with the tract containing the location of the blockhouse and knows its precise location.

This blockhouse is located in West Finley Township, Washington County. To get to it from Pittsburgh you should proceed onto Interstate 70 W and proceed to Exit 2, Claysville. Turn off and proceed 100 feet to Route 40 E. Turn right on Rt. 40 and proceed 1/4 mile to the edge of Claysville. Turn right on State Rt. 231 S and go under Interstate 70. Just beyond the underpass turn right, still on Rt. 231 S, now called Beham Ridge Road. Follow this road four miles to McGuffey Road and proceed 1/2 mile to the lane leading to the house of Mr. & Mrs. Eugene F. Ruperto whose address is 1035 McGuffey Road.

The blockhouse site is 100 feet southwest of the house, adjacent to a present tool shed, and just beyond (south) of a present wooden fence. A stone foundation and one large stepping-stone still remain.

(A, then college student, John Mark Wittkofski, prepared a detailed study of this site as a term paper, a copy of which was given me by Mr. & Mrs. Ruperto, and pertinent information had been taken from that paper.)

The Rev. Doddridge describes this blockhouse as a "large and strong one." The foundation measures twenty-four feet square and a portion of two walls and a corner remain today. The doorway is identifiable by a large stepping stone and is on the western side of the house about ten feet from the northwest corner. It looks toward a spring located about two hundred feet to the west.

Hercules Roney was of Scotch-Irish descent and came to America about 1775 and into this area in 1779. He obtained a Virginia land warrant on December 21, 1779, and the land was surveyed on January 20, 1785. He received his patent (deed) on September 16, 1785, and called the land "Roney's Fancy." He was one of about 2000 people who signed a petition asking the new Federal government to create a new state in this area because of their disgust at the quarreling between Pennsylvania and Virginia over this land. He served with the Washington County Militia and was one of those who followed Col. David Williamson to Gnadenhutten, Ohio, during which the Moravian Indians were massacred. It may be noted that about twenty of those men refused to participate in the killing and whether Roney was one of them is unknown. He also participated in the Crawford Expedition which was defeated near Sandusky, Ohio, in June, 1782, and Roney was one of the lucky ones who managed to evade the Indians and get home. At one time, during a census in 1800 he described his occupation as a weaver.

The most famous incident involving Hercules Roney was his attempt in August, 1789, to come to the assistance of the McIntosh Family, and then to avenge their death. When the oldest McIntosh girl arrived at Roney's Blockhouse with her terrible story, Hercules got together with Duncan McArthur, (later Governor of Ohio), his brother Purcel McArthur, James Armstong, and George Sutherland and headed for the McIntosh home which was about 2 1/4 miles away. There in a field lay Mr. McIntosh and his wife and, scattered on the trial to the house lay the bodies of six children. The men followed the Indian trail down Blockhouse Run and on the south bank of the stream they soon found the body of the McIntosh baby with the family bible lying beside it.

To give an idea of the tenacity of these frontiersmen, Hercules and his men followed this Indian trail all the way down to Moundsville, West Virginia, crossed the Ohio River, and finally lost the trail on the other side of that river. Too bad. If that trail had been found we can be sure that Roney and his men would have followed it all the way to the Mississippi River to get their hands on those Indians. And, if they had caught up with them, I don't think Hercules Roney was planning on leaving any survivors.

Nothing more is known of the activities at this blockhouse. It seems to have served as the fort for at least four families - that of Hercules, his brother James, and their friends Henry Holms and John Bell. All four men came into this area together and owned adjoining properties.

Roney's Blockhouse

This shows the fort site between the lane on the left and the mowed path on the right.

This view looks toward the road from the fort.

One of the original foundation stones at the site.

Campbell's Blockhouse

The site of this blockhouse is in West Finley Township, Washington County, on Blockhouse Run Road.

Its exact location is in the "probable" category.

Mrs. Annalou Blaney Burig grew up on the Blaney farm, where the blockhouse was located, but she was unable to guide us and, instead, gave explicit directions. This places it on Blockhouse Run Road, .6 miles south of Beham Ridge Road and about 200 feet east of the road.

Some confusion is caused by Earle Forrest who, in his "History of Washington County" (p. 258) places it "a mile and a quarter west of Good Intent and two miles south of Elvilla." The problem is that measuring from Good Intent, the road goes southwest for about 3/4 of a mile, then turns right on Blockhouse Run Road and goes straight north. Did Forrest mean "road miles" or "as the crow flies?" Naturally, we have two different locations depending on what he meant, and, significantly, neither is the site identified by Mrs. Burig.

Forrest also refers to "two miles south of Elvilla." That tiny village is shown on old maps as existing at the intersection of Blockhouse Run Road and Beham Ridge Road. Coming south on Blockhouse Run Road for two miles (the road is only 2.1 miles long) does lead to old foundation ruins about thirty feet up on the hillside on the east side of the road. Could these be the foundation ruins of the blockhouse? They just didn't look old enough to us. Again, this is not the Burig site. Also, it is quite hilly terrain here whereas to the north (Burig site) the land is open with more gently rolling hills - a much more logical site for a blockhouse.

To get to this site go down I-70 west to Exit 2, Claysville. Turn off and proceed to US Rt. 40 E. Turn right on Rt. 40 and proceed 1/4 of a mile to the edge of Claysville. Turn right on State Rt. 231 S and go under I-70. Just beyond the underpass turn right, still on Rt. 231 S, now called Beham Ridge Road, and follow this for just about six miles to Blockhouse Run Road. Turn left (south) at this point and proceed .6 miles to the fort site on the left (east) side of the road.

This area was settled by Scotch-Irish immigrants and was known as the "Scotch Settlement." They apparently arrived here about 1785, but the blockhouse was not built until 1790. The terrible killing of the McIntosh family (mother, father, and seven children, earlier described) occurred in August, 1789. This explains why the oldest girl, the sole survivor of that attack, ran to Roney's Fort for help rather than to this blockhouse.

About 1/2 mile down the road, on the west side, is the farm of Mr. John Walbert. Mr. Walbert believes that he has discovered the foundation ruins of the McIntosh cabin which was built over a spring. He took us to the site, at the top of the hill behind his house and about 1/3 mile south. There is a spring at the site, issuing from a gully, and very definite foundation stones on each side and behind it.

Creigh, in his "History of Washington County", p. 57, states: "These settlers had exceedingly hard times. During part of the summer months they were shut up in the blockhouse, and it was with the greatest difficulty and peril they could raise corn sufficient for their families and their stock."

Campbells' Blockhouse

This is the site according to the directions of Mrs. Burig. It is .6 miles south of Beham Ridge Road and on the east side of Blockhouse Run Road.

Mr. Miller and Mr. Gaetano stand on foundation stones at old ruins 2 miles south of Beham Ridge Road and about 30 feet east of Blockhouse Run Road. This site did not appear old enough to be the ruins of the blockhouse, but the distance "squares": with Earle Forrest's directions.

These foundation stones, beside a spring, are reputed to be the ruins of the McIntosh house. They are on the farm of Mr. & Mrs. John Walbert. The McIntosh family was wiped out by Indians except for the oldest daughter.

Lindley's Fort

This fort was one of the best known on the frontier. Its location is well known and had been marked by the Lindley family with the placement of a large granite memorial.

From Washington proceed south on State Rt. 18 to Prosperity. Continue beyond that town 1/2 mile to the site. The granite marker is on the left (east) side of the road and the nearby red brick house was built on the foundation of the fort.

On the hill two hundred yards north is the Upper Ten Mile Presbyterian Church established in 1800 when the fort was still actively used. The name of the church refers to the Ten Mile Creek located beyond the fields about two hundred yards to the west.

This was one of the largest and strongest forts in the area, and it is specifically mentioned by Rev. Doddridge. It must have looked very much like Prickett's Fort. It was built to contain seven families, but so many people came here during Indian raids that small, extra cabins were built outside the stockade walls. It was never attacked directly, but Indians raided the countryside all around it and it must have been in constant use by the surrounding families.

The fort was built about 1773 by Demas Lindley and Jack Cook with help from Caleb and John Lindley, James Draper, and J. McCaugh. They had come from New Jersey with fourteen other Scotch-Irish settlers all of whom settled on Ten Mile Creek. Demas Lindley located on 400 acres of land that were warranted to him on February 5, 1785, surveyed on December 6, 1785, and he gave it the name "Mill Place." He did construct a grist mill on the nearby creek.

The tales abound regarding activities at this fort. Jacob Parkhurst was born and reared about three miles from the fort and, with his family, often "forted up" here. He tells us his mother hated the place "on account of her children running into all manner of mischief and evil." My goodness! That statement certainly tells us something about life in those forts. We know that many children, suddenly brought together in a fort will get into mischief, but what was the "evil" that so disturbed Mrs. Parkhurst?

She was a real frontierswoman - on one occasion, when her husband was gone, an express raced up to tell her Indians were close by and coming. She gathered her children and ran for a mile to a deep ravine where she hid with them for two days. A driving rain finally forced her to take the children - oh so carefully and cautiously - through the woods to Lindley's Fort.

On another occasion her husband and oldest son were gone (didn't Mr. Parkhurst ever stay home!) and word came that Indians were on their way. Three armed men came by to escort the Parkhurst and other families to the fort, but while Mrs. Parkhurst sent her children she stayed behind. She expected that her husband and son were coming soon and she was fearful that no one would be around to warn them of the Indians. She had a rifle and was determined to stay. When the others got to the fort Caleb Lindley decided Mrs. Parkhurst was just plain crazy, mounted his horse, and raced out after her. He did come upon Indians setting up an ambush, turned off the trail, and went around them.

He got to the Parkhurst cabin safely, insisted that Mrs. Parkhurst come with him, mounted her on the back of the horse, and the two of them evaded the Indians and made it back to the fort. Mr. Parkhurst and his son came into the fort that night.

It might be mentioned that the nervy Mrs. Parkhurst was five months pregnant at the time of these goings-on. Tough lady.

As to general events in the neighborhood, we learn that the Davis family was wiped out in one raid "except one son and one daughter;" the Bean family had two girls killed while gathering walnuts with their father; the Carroll family had two boys killed one morning when they went out to get some wood - the rest of the family fled through a cornfield, into some woods, and on to Lindley's; Stephen Carter heard some turkeys gobbling, and suspicious, went out to investigate. He found five Indians in ambush. He held them off while his own family raced for their lives to the fort, then Carter ran to the Parkhurst cabin and got them started and he went on to alert other settlers. Another time a man named Sheridan started for Lindley's but never made it - his body was found about four miles from the fort. John Burns was in Wheeling when Indians raided his cabin. Mrs. Burns grabbed her two children and got away. She walked ten miles with those children to get to Lindley's. That night, at the fort, she gave birth to her third child.

We think we have it rough.

Let us never forget that it is because of these women that we have our country today. They were special.

Lindley's Fort

This large fort extended from the gully on the left beyond the brick house. It was in constant use due to endless Indian raiding.

SITE OF OLD LINDLEY FORT AND STOCKADE BUILT 1770

The descendants of the Lindley family erected this memorial to honor their distant ancestors.

Ten Mile Creek runs along the tree line at the far end of the fields.

Ryerson's Station

The site of this fort has been located in the village of Ryerson's Station in southern Greene County.

To get there proceed down I-79 S to the Waynesburg exit and there turn on to State Rt. 21 W. This leads through Waynesburg and goes on about fifteen miles directly into Ryerson's Station. The fort site is on the west end of the town, on the right (north) side of the road almost directly opposite the South Wheeling Baptist Church. There is a trailer home at the site today.

We do not know when the fort was built except that it was in the 1770's. One story has it that it was built at the direction of Virginia authorities and another that Thomas Ryerson and his neighbors built it. We do know that James Paull commanded a company of Rangers stationed here in 1784 and 1785, and an old muster roll shows Rangers here in the Spring of 1793 under Capt. William Crawford and Capt. James Seals.

Ryerson's Station State Park is near by and the present park office is very close to what was once the Davis cabin. The Indians struck the Davis family as they were having breakfast. Mr. Davis and his two oldest sons were killed as they grabbed for their rifles, four smaller children were killed and scalped before the horrified eyes of their mother and then Mrs. Davis and a young daughter were taken away as prisoners. Shortly thereafter the child was killed; nothing more was ever heard of the mother. One boy, off in the fields working, escaped.

If you would like a very poignant and adventurous trip, go in search of the Crow Rocks - a memorial to the death of the three Crow sisters.

Leaving the fort site continue on Rt. 21 W for 2.4 miles. Turn right (north) onto Dodd-Ridge Road. Follow this for 3.7 miles to a "Y" in the road. Take the left arm of the "Y" and proceed .4 miles over a bridge. There turn left onto a dirt road which follows the creek and go .8 miles. On your right, at the edge of the hillside, you will see the memorial to the Crow sisters and the nearby rock behind which the Indians hid. The four sisters were ambling along the creek on May 1, 1791, when they were captured by two Indians and a renegade white man believed to have been Billy Spicer who was captured when he was eight years old. (See Garard's Fort for the full story.) The three men interrogated the sisters for a while then pulled out their tomahawks and started killing. Christina broke away and escaped. Susanah and Katherine were killed; Elizabeth was beaten down and scalped but she lingered for three days then died.

This memorial is very sad and lonely out there in the woods, off by itself. It's nice to know that someone wants to remember those girls and the awful times they lived in.

As the story goes, Michael Crow lived to avenge the death of his sisters. Some long time afterward he learned that William Spicer was in the neighborhood and he went after him and came home smiling, though he kept silent about what had happened. Suffice it to say that Spicer was never seen again.

Ryerson's Station

The fort stood at this location on the north side of the road.

This looks northwest at the fort site from the South Wheeling Baptist Church.

This view looks east back into the village of Ryerson's Station.

Crow Sisters' Massacre Site

Off in the woods, in a lonely, desolate spot, is this memorial to the killing of three Crow sisters. The rock, behind which the Indians hid, is in the background.

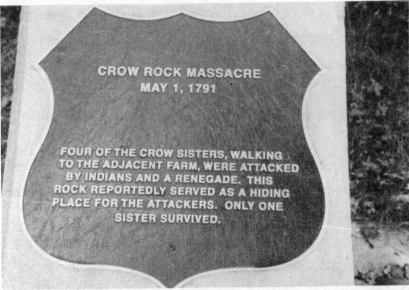

CROW ROCK MASSACRE
MAY 1, 1791

FOUR OF THE CROW SISTERS, WALKING TO THE ADJACENT FARM, WERE ATTACKED BY INDIANS AND A RENEGADE. THIS ROCK REPORTEDLY SERVED AS A HIDING PLACE FOR THE ATTACKERS. ONLY ONE SISTER SURVIVED.

The inscription on the memorial Susanah, Catherine, and Elizabeth were killed. Christina broke away and escaped.

Taken from the rock, this view shows the creek and the path, today a road, along which the girls were strolling that fateful day.

Garard's Fort

The site of this fort is well known and is identified by a state historical marker at the location. It is in Greene County just a few miles east of I-79.

To get to this site proceed south on I-79 to Exit 2 which is identified as the Garard's Fort exit. Turn left (east) on State (Legislative) Rt. 2011 for four miles to the village of Garards Fort. On the east edge of town is the Goshen Baptist Church, well marked, founded by the Rev. Corbly, and .1 miles beyond that is the Garard Fort Cemetery on the left (north) side of the road, and .4 miles beyond that is the fort site on the left (north) side of the road. A white house is at the site today on a small plateau above the road. Muddy Creek, now Whitely Creek, is to the south about 100 feet.

This fort was well used by the nearby settlers and the area was the scene of horrible massacres by the Indians. The killing of the family of the Rev. John Corbly (his wife, an infant, a six year old son, a daughter, and the scalping of two older girls) has been previously recounted, and the Spicer Family was also wiped out by the Indians led by the nefarious, but well-known, Logan. This happened on June 5, 1774. Mr. Spicer was working in the front yard; William, aged nine, was setting traps for squirrels; Mrs. Spicer was in the house; Elizabeth, aged twelve was ironing clothes. Four other children were playing. Logan came with twelve warriors and killed everyone but Elizabeth and her young brother, William. These two ran away and hid but were soon discovered and taken prisoner. Elizabeth came back some years later; William became a "White Indian."

Six dead, two prisoners - another family destroyed.

Logan and his party also killed an old man named Keener on this same day, at a spot about a mile west of the fort. On June 11 a Ranger party from the fort was ambushed and three men killed.

This was a lively place for hostilities.

There is a story that there was a tunnel, stone-lined, leading from a blockhouse at one end of the fort to the side-yard of the present house. This is reputed to have been a secret passage for exit/entry in case the fort was surrounded by Indians.

Among the famous "Draper Manuscripts" (now at the Wisconsin Historical Society, Madison, WI) is a letter dated July 20, 1777, from William Jacobs, at Garard's Fort, which reads:

"Dear Sir:

I am now at Garard's Fort with 12 men only, and am Intirely without Ammunition, and also without my full Quota of men. I hope you will send by Van Sweringen Some Ammunition and flint and as the Times is So Hazardous I hope the men may be ordered to Come here Immediately, as the People are much put to it to get their Harvest up, the creek, and it is not in my power to go on a scout with so few men and leave men to guard the people.

I am Sr Yr Very Hbl Servt:

Wm. Jacobs."

Obviously, militia units were stationed here from time to time.

George Morris, together with Justus and Jonathan Garard, the Rev. John Corbly, and several others came here to settle in the Spring of 1773. They settled on adjoining tracts of land and worked together to build the fort on the land of Jonathan Garard. It is believed that the fort was built either in late 1773 or the early Spring of 1774. It was 100 feet square, had a stockade fence, and is believed to have had two blockhouses at opposite corners - the standard design of a fort at that time.

As has been previously mentioned it was well known and well used in those terrible days.

Garard's Fort

This house marks the location of the fort. It overlooks the highway and the nearby creek which parallels the highway.

This State Historical Marker is along the road at the site.

GARARD'S FORT

Site of frontier refuge in Revolutionary War; station in 1777 of small detachment of Virginia militia. Near here, on Sunday, May 12, 1782, Indians killed the wife and three children of Rev. John Corbly, a Baptist minister.

PENNSYLVANIA HISTORICAL AND MUSEUM COMMISSION

The breadth of the plateau at this spot is shown in this photo. The fort was a large one and would have encompassed a sizable area.

Bibliography

Bakeless, John. <u>America As Seen By Its First Explorers</u>. New York, NY: Dover Publications, 1961.

Billington, Ray Allen. <u>Westward Expansion</u>. New York, NY: The Macmillan Company, 1967.

Buck, Solon J. and Elizabeth Hawthorn Buck. <u>The Planting of Civilization in Western Pennsylvania</u>. University of Pittsburgh Press, 1939.

Craig, Neville B. Ed. <u>The Olden Time, Vol</u>. I. Pittsburgh, Pa.: Dumars & Co., 1846,

Diffenderffer, Frank Ried. <u>The German Immigration Into Pennsylvania</u>. Baltimore, Md.: Genealogical Publishing Co., Inc., 1979).

Doddridge, Joseph. <u>The Settlement and Indian Wars of the Western Parts of Virginia and Pennsylvania, 1763 - 1783</u>. Bowie, Maryland: Heritage Books, Inc., 1988; reprinted in 1912, Pittsburgh, Pa.

Eckert, Allan W. <u>That Dark and Bloody River</u>. New York, NY: Bantam Books, 1995.

Eckert, Allan W. <u>Wilderness Empire</u>. Boston, Mass.: Little, Brown and Company, 1969.

Eckert, Allan W. <u>Wilderness War</u>. Boston, Mass.: Little, Brown and Company, 1978.

Forrest, Earle R. <u>History of Washington County, Pennsylvania</u>. Chicago, Ill.: S.J. Clarke Publishing Company, 1926.

Hamilton, Edward P. ed. <u>Adventure In the Wilderness: The American Journals of Louis Antoine Bougainville 1756 - 1760</u>. Norman, Okla.: Univ. Of Oklahoma Press, 1964.

Harpster, John W. Ed. <u>Pen Pictures of Early Western Pennsylvania</u>. Univ. Of Pittsburgh Press, 1938.

Illick, Joseph E. <u>Colonial Pennsylvania</u>. New York, NY: Charles Scribner's Sons, 1976).

James, Alfred Procter and Charles Morse Stotz. <u>Drums In The Forest</u>. Pittsburgh, Pa.: The Historical Society of Western Pennsylvania, 1958.

Kelley, Jr. , Joseph J. <u>Pennsylvania: The Colonial Years, 1681-1776.</u> Garden City, NY: Doubleday & Company, Inc., 1980.

Kellogg, Louise Phelps, ed. <u>Frontier Retreat on the Upper Ohio</u>. Bowie, Md., Heritage Books, Inc., 1994.

La Crosse, Richard B. Jr. <u>The Frontier Rifleman</u>. Union City, Tenn.: Pioneer Press, 1989.

Leckey, Howard. <u>The Ten Mile Country and Its Pioneer Families</u>. Knightstown, Ind.: Green County Historical Society, 1977.

Lobdell, Jared C. ed. <u>Indian Warfare in Western Pennsylvania and Northern West Virginia at the Time of the American Revolution</u>. Bowie, Md.: Heritage Books, Inc., 1992.

Lough, Glenn D. <u>Now And Long Ago</u>. Morgantown, W.Va.: Morgantown Printing & Binding Co., 1969.

Montgomery, Thomas Lynch (ed.). <u>Frontier Forts of Pennsylvania, Vol. II, 2d ed.</u> Evansville, Ind.: Unigraphic, Inc., 1978, originally published 1916, Harrisburg, Pa..

Parkman, Francis. <u>The Jesuits In North America</u>. Williamstown, Mass.: Corner House Publishers, 1980.

Pouchot, Pierre. <u>Memoirs On the Late War In North America Between France and England, Ed. By Brian Leigh Dunnigan</u>. Youngstown, New York: Old Fort Niagara Association, Inc., 1994.

Rupp, I.D. <u>Early History of Western Pennsylvania</u>. Lewisburg, PA: Wennawoods Publishing, 1995; originally published, 1846, Harrisburg, Pa..

Shimmell, Lewis S. <u>Border Warfare In Pennsylvania</u>. Harrisburg, Pa.: R.L. Myers & Company, 1901.

Sipe, C. Hale. <u>Fort Ligonier and Its Times</u>. Arno Press & The New York Times, 1971.

Sipe, C. Hale. <u>The Indian Wars of Pennsylvania</u>. Lewisburg, Pa..: Wennawoods Publishing, 1995), originally published in 1931, Harrisburg, Pa.

Smith, James. <u>Scoouwa: James Smith's Indian Captivity Narrative</u>. Columbus, Ohio: Ohio Historical Society, 1978.

Stotz, Charles Morse. <u>Outposts of the War for Empire</u>. Pittsburgh, Pa.: Historical Society of Western Pennsylvania, 1985.

Thomas Lynch Montgomery (ed.). <u>Frontier Forts of Pennsylvania, Vol. I, 2d ed</u>. (Evensville, Ind.: Unigraphic, Inc., 1978.

Thwaites, Reuben Gold and Louise Phelps Kellogg, Ed's. <u>Frontier Defense On The Upper Ohio, 1777-1778</u>. Madison, Wis.: Wisconsin Historical Society, 1912.

Thwaites, Reuben Gold and Louise Phelps Kellogg, Ed's. <u>The Revolution On The Upper Ohio, 1775-1777</u>. Port Washington, N.Y.: Kennikat Press, 1908.